CONTENTS

Contents

Contents

Introduction

In 1975 the Bullock Committee reported that,
in their wide and representative sample of secondary
schools, 84.4% of the drama in these schools was
taught as part of the work of the English department and only 9.9% was accounted for by a separate
drama department. There are good reasons for
believing that any survey undertaken in the 1980s
would reveal an even greater imbalance, for at a
time of falling rolls and financial contraction,
as full time drama teachers leave they are not
being replaced, and the responsibility for teaching
drama in the curriculum is falling more and more
squarely on the shoulders of the English department.
Any current survey of English departments would show
that in many cases drama is either not being taught
at all or is being taught erratically or inadequate-
ly, not because of a lack of interest or general
incompetence but because of a feeling of insecurity
and lack of direction: 'Where are we to start?',
'How are we to accommodate drama in the teaching
spaces available to us?', 'How shall we link drama
with our current English activities?'.
    Brian Watkins, a drama authority with his ear
very close to the groundswell of insecurity,
concluded in his recent book 'Drama in Education',

> Drama teaching at all levels in our schools
> is in a state of confusion. This is not
> just because there is considerable disagreement
> about how to teach it, but because there exists
> no universally accepted idea of what it is or
> what is its purpose in education.

This despite the fact that English teachers are in
no doubt about the valuable contribution drama can
make to the teaching of English. There have been

1

those, of course, who have attempted to tie down, to
define drama in education, Brian Watkins included,
but such works have spoken almost entirely to the
small proportion (the Bullock Committee's 9.9%) of
full time drama specialists and to teachers with
access to tailor-made drama spaces. Almost nothing
has been written to support and inform the work of
those teachers who account for the vast majority of
drama taught in schools, and these are teachers of
English who see their drama work as running in
tandem with the English theme, set book, poetry or
projects and who must reconcile educational drama
with sometimes patently inadequate drama teaching
areas. It is little wonder that, given insufficient
guidance both in initial training and from over-
stretched heads of department and advisers, that
drama's vital contribution to language development
is being neglected.

Any book dealing with educational practice in
the 80s and beyond must, if it is to have any
credibility in the eyes of its audience, recognise
the reality of educational cuts and the closing of
ranks over the curricular gaps such cuts expose.
Rail we may and will but the days of expansion, and
particularly expansion in the number of full time
drama teachers, are over and the fight is on, as
John Tomlinson and others have been the first to
realise, to safeguard a lean curriculum, in some
coherent form. At such times it is not enough just
to offer a subject. It must be clear to everyone
involved, teacher and taught, pupil and parent,
customer and community, that there are sound
practical and philosophical reasons for making the
offer and that the product justifies the faith that
all place in it. Thus drama as a medium for learning is not to be used indiscriminately but must be
firmly fixed to our aims for English teaching in
general, and our objectives for a sequence of
lessons in particular.

Drama has never lacked a natural intimacy with
English. Some, myself included, would assert that
it is impossible to teach English adequately without
teaching drama simultaneously. The Bullock Committee
recognised that 'in its close relation to literature
and its inherent shaping powers for speech, drama is
a powerful instrument' in developing the pupil's
powers of communication. 'It warrants the serious
study and professional discussion that are
characteristic of those schools which are using it
so effectively for this purpose'. Precious little
serious study and professional discussion of the

Introduction

kind the Bullock Committee advocated <u>and</u> in a
context which makes such enquiry relevant to the
reality that English teachers, and thus drama
teachers, face has taken place since 1975. This
book hopes to go some way towards filling that gap.

Chapter One

ENGLISH AND DRAMA: THE PERIMETERS AND PARAMETERS

Any cursory and objective appraisal of the
concerns of teachers of English, and teachers of
drama, will immediately reveal shared aims and
shared content. When canvassed, English teachers
define their subject as one which encourages and
develops communication skills, self-expression,
imagination and creativity[1]. These are the key
terms which surface time and time again in the
declared aims of practising teachers. When similarly confronted, teachers of drama reveal similar
concerns, '"developing the child's powers of self-
expression," "developing self-awareness, self-
confidence, encouraging sensitivity and powers of
imagination"'[2]. So far so good, but these shared
concerns are rather vague, insubstantial beings
stated thus naively, for they scarcely hint at the
sometimes contentious debate as to the true nature
of each subject. Any inquiry into the perimeters
and parameters of English, and drama, must thus
back-track in order to discover the means whereby
such self-expression, imagination and creativity
may be revealed in each, in turn.

ENGLISH : DEFINITION AND AIMS

It is a relatively simple matter to add to the
general concerns above, a list of the 'ingredients',
the raw material of English : language and literature broadly, (while acknowledging that the two are
ultimately indivisible), more specifically, poetry,
plays, novels, short stories, and thence the 'skills'
English hopes to develop in reading, writing, talking and listening, including comprehension,
appreciation, fluency, accuracy and the 'basic
skills' of spelling, punctuation, syntax and hand-
writing. No teacher of English, however liberal,

4

English and Drama: The Perimeters and Parameters

however doctrinaire, could categorically exclude
any of these, but time is tight and classroom
priorities must be decided. These priorities,
whether explicit or implicit, have been distilled
by some to produce identifiable schema for English
teaching, notably the basic skills, cultural
heritage, social studies and 'personal growth'
models[3]. The first stresses functional literacy
and is vocational to the extent that it pays
particular attention to those skills of reading,
writing and talking which will fit pupils for work
and leisure beyond school. The social studies
model tends to deal with themes which have as much
interest for the sociologist and anthropologist
as the teacher of English, poverty, delinquency and
crime among them. David Shayer[4] is typical of
those objectors to this extension of the definition
of English when he describes it as 'an attempt
(seemingly) to absorb English work into an unholy
alliance with the social sciences'. The cultural
heritage model stresses, to a greater or lesser
extent, what the Newsom Report[5] described as,
'the civilising experience of contact with great
literature'. We owe one definition of the 'personal growth' model to John Dixon[6] and the Anglo-
American Dartmouth Seminar. This stresses 'the
need to re-examine the learning processes and the
meaning to the individual of what he is doing in
English lessons' and thus sees the needs and
interests of the pupil as of paramount importance.
    There will always be some teachers who are
drawn towards one of these models by the nature of
their clientele. The adult literacy tutor will feel
closer to the basic skills model; the teacher of the
conventional 'A' Level English course will come
closer to the cultural heritage model; the teacher
of English within a general studies or integrated
humanities programme will lean towards the social
studies model. But these are special cases and most,
sensible, teachers of English recognise that any
single model is limited by what it excludes. The
inspired and successful teacher of English will
always be eclectic in philosophy and approach, without confusing the freedom to fit these to the needs
of the pupils and the context with a wishy-washy
decline into irresolution and insecurity. Any
narrow, dogmatic interpretation of English is made
ridiculous by the breadth of the subject, since as
language it encompasses the medium for communication,
in general, and instruction in other school subjects,
in particular. As literature it cannot avoid, even

5

if this was desirable, dipping its fingers into history, politics, science, art, music, to name only a few. The most perfunctory reading of Chaucer, Shakespeare, Swift, Browning, Huxley, Orwell, Bolt and others takes English well beyond even the social studies model. As George Sampson[7] eloquently put it, 'In plain words and in the ordinary sense, English is not a school "subject" at all. It is a condition of school life'. It is ludicrous to insist on a narrow model for English and simultaneously pay due deference to the importance of self-expression, to bolstering habits of wide reading and to encouraging a healthy attitude to the mass media. While it may have been possible for certain, blinkered grammar school teachers of English to insist on the 'cultural heritage' model a decade and a half ago, no teacher of English in a comprehensive school today (and 85% of secondary age pupils are in comprehensive schools) could afford to limit literature to the 'greats' without further alienating already disillusioned or less able pupils. Similarly, an insistence on the practice of the 'basic skills' without balancing this with the reading of the great and the good for enjoyment would be equally limited. I am suggesting, somewhat heretically, that the notion of distinct models only exists or existed in the minds of those grammar school or secondary modern school teachers and department of education lecturers who are or were not required to confront the reality of the comprehensive school's range of abilities, which demands (since survival is sometimes at stake) that teachers constantly rethink their approaches and objectives in the light of the complexity of changing pupils and situations. It is perhaps poetically just that the foreward to the revised edition of John Dixon's 'Growth through English', written by James Squire and James Britton nine years after the conference which inspired the book, should conclude,

> Dartmouth opened with the question, "What is English?", which now seems to us a singularly unrewarding attempt to focus attention on the subject matter of the discipline. The conference responded with the answer, "English is whatever English teachers do" ...What is English? It proves impossible to mark out an area less than the sum total of the planned and unplanned experiences through language by means of which a child gains control of himself and of his

relations with the surrounding world.

With this concluding sentence, we have come full circle from the nebulous concern with creativity and the imagination, which teachers of English and drama obviously share, through a rejection of the unrealistic polarisations of distinct English models, back to something vague to do with language. This last is hardly a convincing foundation for exploring the shared ground between English and drama. The question, 'What is English and what does it hope to do?' is not answered yet. Although we may agree that 'English is whatever English teachers do', that is no help for the majority of teachers who are not charismatic ad-libbers. We all need to know what we are choosing between at the very least, in order to eliminate the possibles, to order priorities, before embarking on a lesson or course of work. We can start by assuming that an eclectic approach to the variety within English teaching must result in proficiency in the basic skills of reading and writing, in communicating intelligibly, must include exposure to a wide range of literature, must allow practice in language use, both written and oral, and particularly the latter and should broaden the intellectual, aesthetic and, we hope, spiritual horizons of each pupil. This last, hints at another debate which affects both English and drama and one which the Calouste Gulbenkian Foundation[8] takes up, 'Some subjects act as umbrella headings under which a number of areas of understanding and experience can be tackled. English not only provides for the practice and understanding of the literary arts but also, through them, for moral education'. The authors of this study wisely do not extend this line of argument too far, and thus avoid the worse excesses of those who claim too much, too immediately for English. George Sampson[9], writing in 1921, forthrightly puts the 'spiritual' claim for English into proportion, 'Let us have no pose or affectation about it. Reading Blake to a class is not going to turn boys into saints'. We can only hope that English and drama help to make our pupils better citizens. We can, and English and drama certainly should, introduce stimuli and set up situations which jolt our pupils into seeing issues from viewpoints other than their own, but there is a difference between this hope and the hyperbole of the 'moral edification' enthusiasts who feel that injections of the 'greats' are to be prescribed to improve the patient.

English and Drama: The Perimeters and Parameters

Peter Doughty[10] suggests that:

> There is no current consensus which expresses
> a majority view of what English ought to be.
> Teachers of English are conspicuous for the
> fact that they seem to talk with as many
> voices as there are contributors to the debate.

But he recognises the apparent paradox that these
many 'voices' co-exist with a shared belief in a
common set of essentials, of shared aims;

> What we find in an English classroom is a
> unique combination of features which are
> themselves nonetheless likely to occur in
> many other English classrooms in combinations
> just as unique... Objectives and aims give
> teachers of English a shared basis for a
> common "theory of English"...

The following distillation of the aims that inform
the best practices of teachers of English is one
with which few will disagree:
English aims to:

Develop the basic means of communication:
talking, writing, reading (and by inference
listening) and thus encourage fluent and
accurate expression, both oral and written.

Widen experience through the exploration of a
wide range of language registers. Encourage
appreciation and experience of the linguistic
demands of different literary types, e.g.
instruction, description, narrative, dialogue,
etc.

Develop the pupil's ability to read with
pleasure, understanding and discrimination,
distinguishing between the valuable and the
second-rate, the genuine and the sham.

Encourage delight in the depth and variety of
English literature, not neglecting the best
and the greatest available.

Extend vocabulary and encourage delight in
words, their meanings, uses and power.

Encourage an informed and tolerant attitude
to the views of others.

Dispel self-consciousness and develop the pupil's confidence to express views openly and coherently.

Allow pupils some control over the course of the lesson in order to develop personal initiative and individual creativity.

Make English meaningful and relevant through its links with life outside school.

This list,[11] which sums up what secondary school teachers of English have in common, discloses in more detail the common ground that English and drama share and can simultaneously develop. Drama should contribute significantly to the realisation of all these aims, but before we can consider the nature of the contribution we must have some idea of what 'drama' is all about, and again this consideration most sensibly begins with a list of 'ingredients', with which few would argue.

DRAMA : DEFINITION AND AIMS

Educational (i.e. curricular drama) encompasses movement, mime, improvisation, the scripted play, theatrical performance and related skills, and theatrical history. Ask the intelligent student or layman an open-ended question such as, 'What do you know about drama?' and he will probably reply, 'Do you mean about what we did in the drama lessons in school, or reading plays, going to the theatre or seeing plays on television?', since these are all, and just a selection of, the facets of drama. There is an obvious distinction between acting out and improvisation in the classroom, and theatrical drama such as a Royal Shakespeare Company performance. Between these two lies a wide grey area of controversy since, as Lynn McGregor[12] suggests, in a chapter significantly entitled 'The controversial nature of drama', the debate about the relationship between these two is, if recent studies are to be believed, even more fiercely fuelled than that regarding the nature of English within the curriculum. The controversy revolves around questions such as, 'Should educational drama concern itself with performance, of any sort, before an audience?', 'To what extent does discussion play a part in drama teaching?' and 'Should drama teaching include a study of theatrical history?'. As with the debate about the true heart of English teaching, these 'controversies' are more apparent to those who stand well back from the reality of day to day teaching. Successful practising teachers of English and drama, while deciding their priorities, have the common sense not to agonise over definitions of educational drama (even if they had the time). The dilemmas they face relate to more practical concerns, which, while they can never be divorced ultimately from aims and perimeters, are bound to an eclectic and pragmatic approach.

It has become commonplace to give the impression that no progress is possible in drama until we can define drama into the ground. Too many books have spent too many pages defining drama on a theoretical and philosophical level, beating off all but their own vacuum-packed interpretation, without showing what drama can amount to in practice, and the responsibility of practitioners for exploiting its breadth to the ends of self-expression, creativity and learning. So we must clear the ground decisively for an examination of what drama can and should be.

Briefly, drama must encapsulate both process and product (as in all the arts) in a continuum which allows room for spontaneity through mime, movement and improvisation and the satisfaction of the polished performance. Somewhere along that continuum perch the school play and theatrical history and they are not to be dogmatically excluded since they are two, albeit minor, elements in educational drama, whose strength lies in its broad emphasis on the process of doing drama, 'the thing done': 'there can be no division between the exploratory drama and the communicative function, theatre. Both employ the same essential dramatic process, but differ in the degree of the constraint attending them[13]'. While the pundits may advocate one approach rather than another, the successful drama teacher knows that the way the 'ingredients' feature in the drama lesson depend less on abstract ideological notions and more on the clientele, context and localised objectives.

If a case can be made for drama, it ought to be sufficiently broadly-based to take in all examples of the work... The essential task is to develop a framework of ideas, a rationale for drama, within which the teacher can begin to explore and develop his own way of working. Stylistic variations arising out of the uniqueness of each teaching situation ought then to

be placed in their proper perspective. They
emerge from individual differences within each
group rather than out of basic differences in
the nature of drama... The important question
here relates to the teacher's specific intentions with this group, at this time and in this
place. If there are different approaches, then
it must be said that there are as many as there
are teachers in schools[14].

BEYOND THE COMMON GROUND

This last, eminently reasonable statement returns
us to a point equivalent to the all-embracing
but ultimately frustrating definition of English
provided by Squire and Britton, fine for those who
know where and what they are at, but disconcerting
for the novice about to embark on drama teaching.
We can come closer to the nature of drama by
expanding the statement which began the preceding
section, by asserting that drama allows participants
the opportunity to act out roles and to use all the
media of communication, the voice, gesture, movement,
so to do. It thus takes what it shares with English,
an emphasis on developing the means of communication,
and extends these means to include all the paralinguistic aids to meaning which take communication
beyond the two dimensional writing and talking to
involve the third dimension of gesture and physical
interaction, thus encouraging active and discriminating observation and listening, which true communication always demands. More specifically drama, as has
been suggested, contributes to the realisation of the
aims for English teaching already stated. Drama
does this by:

Providing opportunities for pupils to practise
a wide range of language registers, thus extending vocabulary, particularly that demanded by
unfamiliar contexts.

Encouraging particular kinds of language use,
essential in the drama process, but too often
neglected in English teaching, e.g. planning,
hypothetical and reviewing talk.

Building confidence, particularly through
group co-operation and the sharing of ideas.

Focussing attention on any area for study,
making the easily forgotten memorable and throw-

11

ing new light on the familiar or cliched.

Furthering appreciation and interpretation of
the written word and stimulating the pupils'
own written work.

Allowing the less conventionally academic pupil
scope for success, thus reorientating all
pupils' notions of areas for success.

Opening up the mass media for inspection and
analysis.

Helping to explore and destroy stereotypes
(particularly sexists and racial ones) through
the imaginative leap that drama always requires.

Thus drama has far more to offer English than simply
a shared interest in the scripted play, which is
where the relationship has too often ended in the
past, in what Education Survey Two[15] described as the
'strong literary element in drama'. Drama reinforces
the aims of English teaching but does not stop there,
just because it is patently not the same as English
and is certainly not its more 'academic' brother's
pale practical shadow, as it has sometimes been
mistakenly portrayed in the past. The difference
between English and drama accounts for the significance and vigour of the contribtuion drama makes to
English teaching. The nature of this difference
can best be explored inversely, that is by looking
at what English amounts to if drama is excluded.

LOST CHANCES : ENGLISH MINUS DRAMA

If drama is excluded then English teachers cannot
claim, as they often do, that English is concerned
with communication in its widest and truest sense,
for without drama's third dimension, communication
in English lessons amounts to a two dimensional
classroom travesty. Even a fleeting glance at a
model for communication suggests how much is
lacking in the interpretation accorded to it in the
conventional classroom.

C O N T E X T

Addressor-message-medium-addressee-interpret-response
ation

C O N T E X T

Many[16] have noted the teacher's monopoly on
communication in the classroom. Chalk and talk
still rules and most of that talk is teacher talk
which is overwhelmingly explanatory and regulatory.
Questions from pupils, unless about trivia, 'How
long does it have to be, Sir?', 'Can I sharpen my
pencil?', are rare and seldom suggest attacking
thinking which goes to the heart of the topic,
'Teachers make most of the communicative moves,
forcing the other "players" to respond rather than
allowing them to launch initiatives of their own[17].'
Far from initiating, pupils wait for teachers to
define the, usually narrow, boundaries within which
choice and initiative are permitted, and when
confused or jaded by the teacher's monopoly of ideas,
of talk, they remain quiet, convincing the teacher
that 'They just can't think for themselves', beginning a vicious circle where the teacher takes even
more control since the pupils apparently cannot be
relied upon or trusted to think for themselves.
Thus one addressor with one kind of message dominates
the addressees, who tend to be treated as a homogeneous mass, and once the audience receive the
message there is scant time and opportunity for
interpretation, let alone response. Not only, as
Barnes and others have demonstrated, do teachers
seldom ask questions which suggest that they are
genuinely interested in the reply and are genuinely
open to all considered responses, but they do not allow
pupils the chance to think about what is being
suggested or asked, to make sense of the teacher's
words and concepts, thus minimising the pupil's
chances of assimilating and accommodating the new
information. Often the noisiest person in the classroom is the teacher, who must seem to the pupils
almost neurotically allergic to the silence which
must inevitably accompany a considered response.
    Of course part of the problem lies in the role
relationship between teacher and pupil. The teacher
will object naturally enough, 'but I know what I
want to impart. My knowledge and experience of what
they need to know are what qualify me as a teacher',
and of course this is both true and necessary. But
if we believe, as we must, that English is about
communication, self-expression, imagination,
creativity, if it is both art and language, opinions
and ideas, then we cannot afford to suggest that
pupils are empty vessels with little or nothing to
contribute to the content and texture of the lesson.
Opinions and thoughts are crystallised through
articulation and we must engineer situations which

allow pupils to contribute their own information and knowledge, and which allow pupils to make the teacher's knowledge 'their own'. This will never be possible where English is presented as simply a succession of undeniable facts about language and literature, nor will it be possible where the teacher's lesson plans assume ideas are always teacher initiated or neglect to see 'English' from each pupil's point of view.

Most pupils see secondary school English, like all other academic subjects, as a solitary activity. The teacher presents the stimulus, each pupil responds individually and simultaneously, doing the same thing with little or no choice. If there is a chance for comparing views, pupils are often not aware of it, since the teacher, solitary himself, completes the exercise by marking the work at home, before returning it at high speed some time later, allowing no scope for leisurely and vital comparison and commendation. If communication is about inter-action, about sharing views with others then in too many cases the only interaction in many classrooms is between the individual pupil and the teacher's red pen. One needs only to monitor the experiences of all but the most extrovert pupils to realise how seldom the teacher talks to them individually or goes to the trouble of constructing a framework in which they can contribute. One drama teacher, quoted by Lynn McGregor[18], makes the point graphically,

> They sit in their desks... they write and listen and do what they are asked and they don't have to <u>work</u> and they don't have to give any <u>ideas</u> and have to share... they might be <u>asked</u> to write an essay, but it's just <u>there</u> and there's no way of participating. But <u>you know</u>, if it wasn't on the timetable as drama, it would be lacking. Getting together to create something. Listening to other people - <u>caring</u> what another person has got to say. I <u>think</u> that is the most important thing.

The Bullock Report phrases it somewhat differently but its conclusion is the same, '...it is our contention that in most schools drama has yet to realise its potential in helping the child to communicate with others, to express his own feelings and thoughts and to gain confidence in a variety of contexts.'

If one addressor is monopolising the addressing, delivering usually only one type of message and allowing insufficient room for interpretation, the context for communication in the classroom builds in its own only too obvious constraints. This is communication like no other communication the pupil indulges in. The physical constraints are obvious; communication takes place for the most part in an arrangement of furniture which militates against the give and take of communication. Pupils usually sit in rows where, while they are only too aware of the teacher's centre front presence, they can only see their neighbours in profile, never face to face, so important if the speaker is to gauge the response of the listener. And, should pupils have the temerity to turn round to see who is talking, to relate the sound and content to the facial expression and pose of the speaker, then the teacher is likely to say wearily, 'Turn round and face the front and listen'. The classroom is arranged to facilitate control of a large number of individuals but the convenient arrangement of rows of desks facing the front is at odds with meaningful and uninhibited discussion. Any analysis of the process of communication cannot ignore the paralinguistic accompaniments to the spoken word; try communicating to someone you cannot see and it will soon become apparent how dependent we are on facial set and associated gestures to explain the words. When pupils are behind desks they are handicapped communicators since scope for movement is limited.

The teacher, because of his central position, must process and distil all contributions before they are relayed to the rest of the class. Teachers tend habitually to preface responses to answers with, 'You mean that...', 'What you're trying to say is...', not only because they are reinforcing the importance of the message but because this is the only way of relaying a message directed at the only face the pupil can see to all the other faces that only the teacher can see. There are very good reasons for asking pupils to sit behind desks, never to leave their positions, if it is assumed that all or almost all ideas will come from the teacher and if communication is interpreted almost solely as writing, but no self-respecting English teacher could afford to limit his interpretation to this extent. True, pupils will be finally examined almost entirely in their use of the written word rather than the spoken word, but this is just one example of how the examination system is at odds with how we assess each other in life. We communicate and thus judge each other's powers of articulation almost wholly via the spoken word; even those working in the most word intensive businesses, in schools and universities, do relatively little writing beyond the formal essay assignments required of them.

Thus we have English classrooms which are actively at odds with our declared aims of encouraging and developing informed opinion and self-expression. But they are often 'ecologically' at odds too, for where interaction assumes that pupils talk almost exclusively to and via the teacher and given that, with a single teacher and large classes the mathematical chances of the individual contributing might allow no more than two seconds per head per lesson, then the pressure is on for pupils to get it right first time; that is to talk 'in best'. There is little time for the tentative, hypothetical, the 'What if...?', 'But I wonder...', 'I'm not sure that...', when the implication is that time is short and all pupils are individually competing to get the attention of the only important person in the room. The expression of opinion outside the classroom usually assumes a fairly relaxed atmosphere which is not a narrow duologue but an interchange of views among many. True, there will still be competition to find space for one's own views, but the guillotine will not be so obvious and threatening. Pupils will only be able to make sense of new knowledge and incoming ideas if they are given the opportunity to talk 'expressively', spontaneously and anecdotally.

How can drama redress the balance and contribute to a more meaningful, less distorted and limited interpretation of 'communication' in the classroom? To start with, drama is a co-operative venture since

> It involves being able to learn to contribute, to accept and share other people's ideas, to build on them and come to corporate decisions about which ideas are thought to be appropriate to what the children want to explore and also whether adequate forms of expression can be found in which to say them. Drama can give children the opportunity to communicate between themselves and to arrive at corporate and positive decisions about what to do and how to do it[19].

That is, drama returns the initiative to pupils; it makes the important first step of conceiving that they have something to contribute and that any contribution need not be a solitary one, that it is no form of 'cheating' to learn from one's peers and to pool ideas and decide priorities as a group. Drama provides a context for learning, not simply about imaginary situations and real events, but fundamentally about relationships, about each other, and this gets to the heart of communication,

> More than one child has looked forward to periods of drama as that time when "you get to know people". There still seems to be a surprising amount of time in school when it is not permitted to talk to others or meet people and form relationships[20]

Thus drama shifts the emphasis from subject (examination) learning to social education in a school curriculum where opportunities for co-operation and collaboration are rare, thus barring so many valuable types of language use, 'Some learning can go on without the help of others, but learning to use language and learning to think necessarily depend on interaction with other people[21]'.
    It is in part drama's spontaneity, its emphasis on the unfolding of conversation, action, events in the present, that allow insights and language experiences which seldom see the light of day in the classroom where the lesson has been pre-processed and pre-packaged by the teacher, where routine tasks rule and there are few surprises, 'It is this very immediacy of the process which can lead children to insights and discoveries they might not otherwise experience'[22]. Drama allows opportunities for invention just because the language it employs is so much broader than the routine language of the classroom, particularly so when compared with the formal written tasks, typically demanded of pupils. 'There appears to be an important distinction between children's language in improvised drama and that of most of their written work. The one is open-ended, volatile, and incremental in structure and idiom; the other is relatively closed and formalistic'[23]. Conventional teaching methods, based as they are on the supremacy of the written word in deciding the calibre of pupils, tend to confirm the status quo of pupil achievement. They tend to reinforce the pupil's static picture of himself as bright -

17

average - 'thick'. They allow few opportunities
for pupils surprising themselves into success, in
the way Billy Caspar does in 'A Kestrel for a
Knave'. Drama, at its best, guarantees the possibility that all pupils will be able to shine in
some way, since the stress swings away from
'technical' written accuracy to what works in the
context, to the depth of feeling suggested by a
performance, to the ability to move, entertain,
organise. Drama recognises talents that most lessons
rarely do, and while it does not assume that everyone is an actor, it recognises that everyone has a
huge fund of experienced feeling and action on which
to draw.
      Drama thus broadens the range of language in
the classroom, extending it beyond teacher talk and
the written assignment, allowing success to the less
conventionally academic pupil and reinvigorating
language use generally. But ideally it goes further
since, to a greater or lesser extent it rewrites
role relationships between teacher and taught.
There can no longer be one right answer, one person
with a monopoly on the right interpretation, since
the concern is now less with product than with
process, the journey rather than the terminus. Seen
in this light, drama becomes a means for learning, a
teaching method which states, these are the perimeters for the situation, act out and justify your
decisions and responses as much for yourselves as
for the teacher. It says, in effect, all answers
are possible if they make sense to you and if you
can justify them. Thus, the language which is used
to justify or describe a dramatic interpretation is
as important as the language which is employed in
the acting out. Pupils are not commonly called upon
to justify their views, or don't normally care to
in classrooms that seem to deny that pupils could
legitimately hold and defend a minority view which
differs from the teacher's own. Acting out in role
and justifying the assumed character's actions is
also safer for many pupils than explaining one's
opinions as oneself in the usual classroom context
with all its role reverberations and inhibitions.
The pupil who is speaking in role, or of an assumed
role, has the security, the emotional prop, of being
at one remove from 'reality'; he is speaking from
beneath the skin of another, talking in terms of
'I think he would have said it because...', 'As a
rate'paying member of this community I...'.
      It is impossible to travel far down this road
without confronting concepts like intolerance,

18

ethics, 'truth' and it is part of drama's strength
that it demonstrates the ephemeral and partial
nature of truth, that the medium may well decide the
message and that we are at the mercy of those who
decide which version of the truth reaches us. Thus
drama opens up the mass media for critical appraisal,
since television, radio, the press and films are in
many senses dramatic themselves, conscious perform-
ances which manipulate language, and with their own
leading protagonists. While it is dangerous to
claim too much for the civilising effect of great
literature, it may not be too arrogant to claim that
drama, by displaying the possibilities of presentation and interpretation, is taking the important
first step of identifying the options for behaviour.
Classroom debate may then decide to what extent a
particular course of action is the 'right' one and
in whose terms, 'An education which sets out to help
young people make sense of and contribute to the
world in which they live, must be concerned with
helping to investigate their own values and those
of others'[24].

Drama, at its best, takes us a long and valuable way from the serried rows of desks and the
passive recipients of the teacher's knowledge. But
any departure from the norm may be hard won and will
inevitably demand certain prerequisites if 'three
dimensional' communication is to take place. It may
require not less than a change in the climate for
learning,

> ...we would do well to heed the results of
> research which argues that only in class-
> rooms where there is an emphasis on self-
> directed and self initiated work... will
> there be any departure from the pressures
> of conformity, convention and repetition
> which characterise so much work in our
> schools at present.[25]

This does not of course presume individualised
programme learning, nor an indisciplined, 'What
do you want to do?' approach. It suggests that the
teacher should rethink his intentions and ways of
going about fulfilling these and, significantly,
decide what impression is being left in the minds of
individuals as to the nature of English teaching.
If this revolves around arid chapter summaries,
illogical language exercises, the formal essay, then
we have hardly progressed beyond the elementary
school syllabus. This is the travesty of English

teaching that the Newsom Report described and as
such it does not come close to developing the
communication skills, imaginative flair and creativity close to the hearts of English and drama teachers
Thus we cannot move off from drama until we have
decided what we are moving off from, and the links
and the rationale must be ovious to our pupils as
well as ourselves:

An apparently sudden leap from the course book
exercise to the drama lesson without rhyme or reason
will probably be counter-productive as the drama will
appear little more than an aberration or fill-in to
pupils who are naturally unaware of any link, and,
more practically, are used to a classroom where
passivity is next to godliness:

> If members of the English department combine a
> willingness to listen to anything their young
> people have to say with a respect for the
> traditions of English literature, there is a
> basis for a common course between English and
> drama. But if the English department is mostly
> concerned with syntax, spelling, presentation,
> critical analysis, and textual sophistries, the
> drama teacher had better make common cause with
> his own shadow.[26]

Thus the extent to which we link English and drama
will depend on our interpretation of 'English' and
the more enlightened our interpretation the more we
can expect of drama's contribution to English teaching.

Any such reappraisal of our interpretation of
English teaching should not rest solely with the
individual teacher. There is a departmental
responsibility to discuss the role of drama in
English teaching and to facilitate its inclusion in
the English timetable. As the Bullock Report noted,

> Whatever view is taken of improvised drama by
> heads of English departments, there is too
> rarely any construction or detailed discussion
> of its place in English teaching. Too little
> thought has been given to the various possible
> organisational models by which drama can be
> incorporated into a school timetable.

The national state of drama teaching is a bleak one
where three quarters of all drama taught in secondary
schools is taken by teachers of English who lack the
essential guidance necessary if drama is to make its

potential for language development, in particular,
felt. If charity begins at home so does in-service
training, particularly in a decade in which the
chances for L.E.A. funded external in-service
education courses will be thin on the ground. This
can begin modestly through the pooling of ideas and
the exploration of specialist interests where they
arise; it may mean learning from the successes and
failures of those who have tried to incorporate drama
work in their English teaching, or making the best
possible use of the experiences of those rare fortunate colleagues who have had some drama training or
who have been able to attend secondary drama courses.
It will mean assessing the facilities available for
drama, whether in classroom or hall, and where, in a
minority of schools, a separate drama department
exists, it will require liaison, for drama within
the English department and drama as a distinct
subject area can fruitfully co-exist, as the Bullock Report recognised. The need for departmental
analysis and action is great and immediate if drama
is not rapidly to become an endangered species, at a
time when each curriculum survey which appears re-
emphasises the extent to which spending cuts are
eating into its existence as a separate school subject.

Any successful linking of English and drama of
the kind envisaged above requires:

> Knowledge of the nature of both, and specifi-
> cally the constants, the parameters, which bind
> them most closely.

> Knowledge of the uses to which drama can be put
> in achieving English objectives, and of the way
> English and drama work can co-exist and develop.

> A realisation of the implications, both for
> classroom relationships and classroom organi-
> sation, of any such linking.

The first of these requirements has provided the
substance for this introductory chapter; the remainder, and greater part of this book will deal with
the practical and organisational factors involved in
developing the relationship between English and drama.

NOTES

1. See, for example, Philip Taylor, <u>How Teachers Plan Their Courses</u> (N.F.E.R., 1970).

2. See: Lynn McGregor, Maggie Tate and Ken Robinson, Learning through Drama, Schools Council Drama Teaching Project (10-16) (Heinemann, 1977).

3. See: John Dixon, Growth through English: set in the perspective of the seventies (Oxford University Press, 1975), for a fuller description of these models.

4. David Shayer, The Teaching of English in Schools 1900-70 (Routledge and Kegan Paul, 1972).

5. Ministry of Education, The Newson Report, Half our Future (H.M.S.O., 1963)

6. See 3.

7. George Sampson, English for the English (Cambridge at the University Press, 1921).

8. The Arts in Schools: Principles, Practice and Provision (The Calouste Gulbenkian Foundation, 1982).

9. See 7.

10. Peter Doughty, Language, 'English' and the Curriculum (Arnold, 1974).

11. See also: Tricia Evans, Teaching English (Croom Helm, 1982), Chapter One.

12. Lynn McGregor, Developments in Drama Teaching (Open Books, 1976).

13. Brian Watkins, Drama and Education (Batsford, 1981).

14. See 2.

15. D.E.S., Drama: Education Survey 2 (H.M.S.O. 1968).

16. See, for example, Douglas Barnes, 'Language in the Secondary Classroom', in Douglas Barnes, Jame Britton and Harold Rosen, Language, the Learner and the School (Penguin, 1969).
Edmund Amidon and John Hough (eds.), Interaction Analysis: Theory, Research and Application (Addison-Wesley, 1967).
Arno Bellack et al, The Language of the Classroom (College Press, 1966).

17. A.D. Edwards and V.J. Furlong, The Language of Teaching (Heinemann, 1978).

18. See 12.

19. See 2.

20. John Hodgson, 'Improvisation and Literature in Nigel Dodd and Winifred Hickson (eds.), Drama and Theatre in Education (Heinemann, 1971).

21. Joan Tough, Talk for Teaching and Learning: Schools Council Communication Skills Project 7-13 (Ward Lock Educational, 1979).

22. See 2.

23. D.E.S., The Bullock Report, A Language for Life (H.M.S.O., 1975).

24. See 8.
25. Ibid.
26. John Allen, <u>Drama in Schools: Its Theory</u>
and Practice (Heinemann, 1979).

Chapter Two

MODEST BEGINNINGS

A CLIMATE FOR DRAMA

Armed with a knowledge of what drama can contribute
to the teaching of English, we must next consider
the emotional and physical climate and context in
which drama is to take place. This entails consideration of an appropriate starting time, appropriate
starting points and the physical environment for
drama. This is to put the preliminaries at their
simplest, for any consideration of a starting point
or time involves a level-headed appraisal of what
the teacher must be, and where the pupils and teacher have arrived in terms of classroom relationships.
     The prerequisites for any constructive drama
work are: security and trust, interest and relevance,
confidence and control. These are all nebulous concepts and need spelling out in classroom terms. Security and its associates, trust and respect, suggest
that pupils are prepared to take risks, in giving
opinions, in taking the stage, because the audience
for this in the past has been both supportive and
discerning. Security suggests that pupils will not
flinch at the prospect of working with a group of
pupils they would not normally count as their friends
Confidence comes from knowing that the teacher will
be able to reimpose silence, to deflect tension with
a well-placed joke, or motivate the less co-operative
to contribute to group work. It comes from self-
knowledge and group-knowledge, from knowing that
failure and foolishness are temporary states which
will not fuel long term grudges on the part of
colleagues or teacher. Progress will only really be
possible where the teacher knows the class, its
changing friendship patterns, individuals' interests
and thresholds for boredom or tension. Such knowledge is not assimilated automatically over a period

24

of time; it is the accumulated product of careful observation from many moments, both within and outside lesson time. Trust comes from believing in the teacher's demands, feeling that there is a master plan in which the current task takes its place, that instructions will not suddenly change arbitrarily, and that the teacher means what he says. Significantly, it means understanding the rules of the game; some of these will be general rules which hold good for any context: snide remarks are always wrong, sabotaging the work of another is indefensible. Others are custom made for the circumstances: 'Communicate in whispers, since no one else must hear', 'Do this in slow motion in order to emphasise the precision of the movements'. Adherence to such rules will be encouraged where the teacher trusts pupils with the rationale which determines these, 'I'm asking you to do it this way because...', 'What rules do you think we need to devise in order to help the work along?' and of course where pupils' own ideas are invited and used.

From such trust, security and mutual respect will come self-confidence, but in the context of English and drama this implies something more systematic than a general sense of well-being. It suggests assurance in the use of those techniques that drama demands of its students:

> The ability to work alone, showing personal initiative in devising, planning and developing ideas.

> The ability to co-operate as part of a group, at times submerging ego and personal ambition in the interests of group success.

> The ability to find the best possible means for implementing a plan.

> The ability to speak clearly and coherently, with an eye to the nature of the message and the audience.

> The ability to listen attentively and to discuss one's own work and the work of others, in a sensitive and constructive manner.

Pupils of any age need to have gone some way in developing these skills in the classroom, before using drama, in its fullest sense, to develop them still further. It may seem paradoxical to emphasise drama's contribution to the development of these skills and then insist that pupils practise them, before launching into drama work where the props of chairs and desks are missing, but this is simply the equivalent of the trainee pilot manipulating the controls while the plane is still reassuringly on the runway. All the skills listed are important in English learning whether drama is to play a part or not, and we must engineer opportunities for their development.

While we must allow pupils to develop drama skills, we will also need to practise these role options which drama will require of us if it is not to stultify on a single track. The class will already be familiar with the teacher standing at the front and leading from the front. This, as the preceding chapter suggested, presents the teacher as director and processor of all that goes on. This role will remain important in drama work, but if initiative is to be returned to individuals then the teacher will need to be more flexible in the adoption of roles. We will at times be silent observer, fellow actor, one among equals; we will need to play devil's advocate, sometimes entering the scene, improvisation or discussion, in role and challenging the group to respond to our assumed identity. At times we will need to pretend total ignorance in order to devolve all responsibility for planning and implementation; at times it may be more effective to play the part of the frustrated director jolting his actors into action with a well placed order or time limit. A sudden shift from the single directorial role to a variety of roles will prove difficult for the teacher and perplexing for the class who will probably react with embarrassment if the teacher enters an improvisation as a fellow character without warning. Thus explanation and the sharing of options is needed, and pupils can be trusted with the knowledge that the teacher on this occasion, for these reasons, will be adopting this particular role.

A SPACE FOR DRAMA

Having prepared the climate in which drama can flourish, having established a working relationship in English lessons that provides a springboard for less physically constricted drama work, other pressing concerns emerge, 'When shall we do it?', 'Where shall we do it?' and 'Where shall we start?'.

As primary school class teachers have long

proved, drama does not necessarily need a time slot
to call its own; some of the most valuable work
develops spontaneously from English (and humanities)
work. This may mean trying out a monologue when
inspiration strikes or a sudden shifting of furniture
in order to recreate a juvenile court. This is
obviously made easier where the classroom is large
enough to provide adequate space with the desks and
chairs stacked against the walls, but there are
very few classrooms which are so small as to rule
out drama work of any sort and the lack of space can,
while cramping pupils physically, free them mentally
by providing a familiar and reassuring base from
which to work. A restricted space will inevitably
rule out extravagant movement but it may challenge
teacher and pupils to make the best possible use of
the space available,

> The venue, the environment, the size and nature
> of the available space can affect profoundly
> the nature of the work that can be undertaken.
> I recall the day I first realised that the
> biggest space available is not necessarily the
> most suitable.[1]

Indeed the classroom that pupils know is often the
best place to begin, with sorties to the school hall
as and when it is appropriate and available. Forward planning is essential if the best possible use
it to be made of the school hall. If the department
believes in the importance of drama then the Head
of English should liaise with the timetabler and
other interested parties to share its use, so that
English staff who can make good use of it have access at least once a week. Once this is written into
the English timetable then class and teacher can work
towards ideas and themes which are suited to a large
open space, without making the dangerous assumption
that once available it must be used, whatever the
cost. Large open spaces, whether the school hall
or great outdoors, can be particularly threatening
or distracting to insecure or inexperienced drama
students and can lead to two polarised reactions,
the 'limpet' one where pupils huddle at the perimeters or on anything that remotely resembles a
seat, and the 'liberated' reaction where younger
pupils race around like freed dray horses, investigating and delighting in areas and equipment which
are normally forbidden.
    While it is preferable to have a space which is
large enough to allow all sorts of movement and any

kind of noise, many kinds of drama work do not
require great space for strenuous movement and it
is a myth to suppose that drama always needs to be
noisy. Planning talk, review, many scenes and of
course mime are, or can be, quiet activities. The
sensible teacher of drama soon learns to match objectives to the facilities available; if there are
a large number of chairs they are used as an asset
rather than seen as an insurmountable liability,
if floor space is limited then the area for development becomes the summit meeting rather than the actual confrontation.

STARTING POINTS

Drama lies close to the surface in the everyday course of communication, interaction and play. A couple of ciruits of the playground during the dinner
break will reveal the adroitness of many pupils in
imitating each other and celebrities and their
skills in demonstrating their meaning through mime.
Time and time again in the infant and junior school
playground you will hear, 'Now I'll be the leader
and you be the...' and 'What if we pretend that..?'
Of course such acting out, such play, is rambling
and indisciplined but it is the raw material from
which plots, stories and plays are made. It allows
scope for the hypothetical, 'What if...' which is
so important in producing any kind of convincing
narrative. So in allowing time for drama in school
we are not introducing something that is new and
unfamiliar but are legitimising and channelling
talents which are already apparent outside the class
room.
     All the departure points suggested in this
chapter are deliberately unambitious ones, starting
with 'where the pupils are at'. We need to trust
our instincts and our knowledge of our pupils and
certainly should not be blinded by notions of what
drama should be, at any cost. More ambitious
schemes can come later, but in these early days we
need feel no guilt at directing the course of the
work, at giving pupils narrow scope in which to work
and at putting the emphasis on quiet and controlled
work, which seeks to perfect basic techniques, befor
letting out the imaginative reins.
     Starting points for drama are to be found in al
the stimuli, materials and work to be found in the
English classroom; the story written for homework,
the narrative poem, the radio programme, the prepared speech, the group discussion, the reading alou

of a piece of conversation from the class reader.
All these can be exploited with the minimum moving
of furniture and certainly without a mass exit to
the hall. Any such exploitation assumes that the
class is generally interested in the piece of work
and that they are able to use their voices expressively and in a variety of ways. Any attempt to vary
the monotone which tends to dominate teacher explanation and pupil responses will take us closer to
role play and characterisation and will help pupils
to identify and develop a repertoire of voices which
will be important when it comes to acting out or
when describing another actor's interpretation of a
role. Any experimentation in intonation, in tone,
should be accompanied by a parallel gain in vocabulary. 'He said it in a nostalgic way...', 'I thought
his reading of the speech was too clipped and decisive to fit what we know of him elsewhere...', 'He
turned a statement into a threat'.

Expressive Speech

Before a pupil of any age can take on a role he must
be aware of what his voice is capable, its range and
resources. One starting point is to ask pupils,
perhaps working in pairs or groups, to list as many
synonyms as possible for '...said' (pupils to select
their own subject). A thesaurus is obviously a
help in supplementing pupils' own suggestions and
the final list can form a useful and attractive
classroom display. Pupils can then devise lines
which are open to as many readings as possible,
which can be barked, snapped, queried, recited,
murmured, spluttered and so forth, lines such as
'It's the only thing for it', 'I'm not the one who
ought to do it'. Pupils can practise saying their
lines to each other, using their synonyms to direct
the change of tone for each new interpretation and
can go on to develop this by responding to the implication suggested by the tone of their partner's first
line:
>   'I'm the one who ought to do it'. (Challenging)
>   'I don't see why, you're shorter than I
>   am'. (Querulously)
and can then justify their chosen response. This
may develop into a dialogue which gradually reveals
its context, much as the opening conversation in a
novel might disclose important details of location,
and character status, appearance and personality.
Having experimented with tone, pupils can manipulate
stress, placing the stress on different words or
syllables in their original lines and describing the

effects of these changes. This should accompany
an analysis of key terms, tone, intonation, pitch,
rhythm and stress and of key questions, for example,
what makes a question a question, an imperative an
imperative or a threat a threat. Pupils can experiment with different stress patterns in their readings
of a brief piece of dialogue, either their own or
that suggested by the teacher. They can then anno-
tate the bare bones of a piece of dialogue using
alternative stage instructions, describing the
possible different contexts and personalities who
will inevitably say the same lines in quite different ways. Pupils can take turns at being the director, instructing their colleagues to interpret their
words in a particular way. This could be accompanied by the annotation and interpretation of an extract of conversation from the class reader, where
little help is provided by the author as to how the
lines should be said.

Associated with these simple exercises are many
more which seek to focus attention on the capabilities of the voice, even when the context for communication is a deliberately circumscribed one: A
must answer a question from B using only yes or no
or mmm to suggest a whole range of responses; a
pupil must suggest to his audience the content of a
telephone conversation through what they hear of his
responses; A and B have a conversation using only
one word each, perhaps tripe and onions, bangers
and mash or two words of their own choice. This
last can extend to carrying out specific tasks using
only these two words, perhaps giving directions or
instructions, gossiping about a third party who is
not far away, a doctor examining a patient with a
mystery complaint or a vicar blessing the congreg-
ation at the close of the service.

Once pupils have found their feet through coll-
aborative work in pairs they should have the confidence to move from dialogue to monologue. Both writ
ing and performing these will prove a greater challenge since the writer and performer will be solely
responsible for keeping the audience's interest and
attention. Sometimes it helps if pupils listen to
famous monologues, particularly those of Joyce
Grenfell, Stanley Holloway and Peter Cook, and the
patter of stand-up comedians. Older pupils may read
Browning's dramatic monologues and the more accessible of Shakespeare's soliloquies, though these may
inhibit those who are better left to devising their
own styles rather than aping those of their betters.
Many pupils will need easing into the monologue, and

here the running commentary is particularly useful
since it encourages the development of descriptive
powers and forces pupils, particularly where the
final product is intended for recording, to anticipate and account for their audience's needs, if the
scene is to be revealed as vividly and graphically
as possible. It is also a type of monologue which
is immediately familiar to all pupils, in a way
that the soliloquy is not. Radio is full of the
running commentary as too are the weekend sports
grandstands, and pupils will be familiar with racing,
football and show jumping comentators' attempts to
convey something of the excitement and colour
of the event. Pupils can start by providing a running commentary for a routine domestic task, such as
making and serving a pot of tea or fitting a plug,
as if for an audience who are totally ignorant of
such matters. The task of course becomes more demanding if it is assumed that the audience cannot
see any sort of demonstration. This might develop
into 'An eye-witness view of 2BD's English lesson'
recorded for alien viewing via satellite. This
brief should encourage the commentator to explain,
without tedious detail, those facets of classroom
work and pupil-teacher relationships which an alien
might find bewildering, amusing or outrageous (in
the same way that a baldly objective description of
a game of golf can be made to appear bizarre or
hilarious). The task becomes more challenging when
certain styles or tones are required, 'Approach the
scene as though it is a sporting event', 'Devise
your commentary as though the programme will form
part of a natural history series', 'Try to suggest
through your commentary that the classroom is little
more than an exercise in young humanoid bashing'.
Running commentary does not of course need to be in
the present tense; it may look to the past or the
future, techniques sometimes employed by satirists
to deflate the pretensions of the pompous or apparently powerful.
    Such exercises lead naturally into an invest-
igation of the important part a narrator can play
in dramatic performance, freeing actors to mime an
accompaniment to the narration or reinforcing the
outline through their own words and actions. At
times the narration will make enactment almost redun-
dant through the colour and vigour of the words and
at this point the commentary moves into the realms
of monologue, where the actors people our minds,
rather than the stage. A monologue can perform
many functions: it can reveal the thoughts of the

speaker at one particular moment; it can reveal the speaker's perception of his life thus far; it can justify a particularly outrageous course of action or, as in an interview, present a generally favourable view of the speaker. A monologue can be an apparently, or really spontaneous account of an event, or feeling; it can delve deeper into the stream of consciousness to produce a rush of words which only have any coherence through their importance for that speaker at the moment of utterance. Pupils usually find it easiest to devise their monologues given the security of a framework,

> You each have a card which gives the name and certain personal details of your character. Fill these details out with any more which should add interest. Writing in the first person, "I", prepare a brief introduction for your audience explaining who you are, something of your background, experience, habits, opinions and interests. Try to write it as you think your character would.

Having amassed relevant and interesting information, pupils can adopt a speaking style, accent, dialect, pitch and intonation, which can be tested out by reading the speech to a colleague, before using it (without of course learning it by heart) as a basis for a performed monologue which might form the prelude to playmaking, improvisation or taping.

Question and Answer

'Question and answer' takes us into the realm of dialogue, interview and interrogation, and provides another means of tipping speech work into full blown drama work. Obviously this route works best where the class have always been encouraged to show initiative by asking questions and by attacking any written work they are currently studying. Teachers who suggest, 'Now what are the questions we should be posing in order to understand this?' will find pupils more ready to frame and answer their own questions, a readiness which will be missing where the class has become used to an automatic move to the course book's questions. Pupils should be practised in questioning each other, perhaps after a prepared speech or following the opposer's and proposer's speeches in a class debate. This should help to develop those skills of selection, presentation, and of course listening, which will be needed when guest speakers visit the classroom: the policeman, local

journalist, poet or councillor. Such opportunities
should give pupils the confidence to question certain interpretations of a play or part, whether
privately or publicly, and should introduce a critical framework for consideration of what is, in television and radio, a form of dramatic performance,
the interview. A game like 'Twenty Questions' will
emphasise the necessity of making every question
count, of using words clearly and unambiguously, and
from here pupils can select a celebrity and devise
no more than ten questions which they would want
their choice to answer. Some initial research may
be needed and pupils will need to anticipate the
sort of answers they may receive and possible
shifts of direction, in order to avoid a dead end.
In the case of a local celebrity the dummy run
may be followed by the real thing. More modestly,
pupils can interview each other, and not just their
best friends; trying to dig out answers to questions
which reveal facets of the interviewee's personality,
interests or talents not formerly realised by the
interviewer.

Such exercises also test pupils' abilities to
think and react quickly, skills which will be important in improvisation where meanings, characters and
relationships are negotiated and developed in action,
in the present. There are other, sometimes simpler
exercises, which can be used to develop these skills
and to tip speech work into drama: A answers B's
question without using 'Yes' or 'No'; A answers B's
question with a brazen untruth, as convincingly as
possible with an elaborated reply, e.g. 'Do you
attend X school?' 'No, I've been a nun in this
enclosed order for the past eleven years now...'.
This may lead into simple pair scenes where A confronts B with a question which must be answered as
convincingly as possible so that B evades the
accusation, 'You've been borrowing my bike again
haven't you?' 'Karen says you went out with my Pete
on Tuesday' and thence into 'What time do you call
this to be coming in of an evening?' Pairs can
contrast reactions to this, facetious, submissive,
angry, conciliatory, sarcastic, and can extend this
single and simple response so that the accused and
accusor change their stances and thus their tones
of voice in the course of the confrontation.

It is worth emphasising here, as it will need
re-emphasising throughout the book, that these are
only initial ideas to be introduced by the teacher.
Drama teachers have always found that some of the
best ideas have come from pupils, often tacitly

expressed as, 'That's O.K. but we think our ideas's
even better', and pupils suggestions will frequently
be better just because they reflect personal issues
of particular relevance at the time. This does not
of course mean that any suggestion goes; the teacher
must remain the final arbiter, but pupil ideas,
particularly those expressed at the end of the
lesson, 'Our group thought it would be a good idea
if we did something on...', can be kept in cold
storage to be thawed out when the moment is right
and with due praise paid to those who conceived the
idea.

Reading Aloud

For those pupils with reading problems it will
always be safest to devise routes from English into
drama which do not involve too much reading aloud,
but for those who are fluent readers the play reading and the play text provide an obvious link between the two. This is a central concern which later
chapters will consider in greater detail; for the
purposes of this chapter it is sufficient to chart
the most obvious ways in which play reading may tip
into drama. This ideally assumes that most pupils
are not merely fluent readers but have been encouraged to explore the full repertoire of tone and
pitch, perhaps using some of the exercises suggested
earlier. At the very least it presumes that the
teacher knows the class well enough to know which
reading parts best suit those who volunteer or are
invited to read. There is little point expecting
pupils suddenly to discover expressive voices for
play reading if they have never been allowed to use
their voices expressively in any other context, and
especially where the teacher has suggested, through
monopolising reading, that he is the only one who
can make this come alive. True, there are pupils
who are loath to risk embarrassment and peer group
disapproval by volunteering to read a part, but
many of these, including older and notoriously
'apathetic' students are happy to perform where the
speeches are interesting, not too long and the
vocabulary not over demanding. It is up to the
teacher to seek out plays, particularly one acters
which contain shorter parts (see, for example, the
Spirals series, Hutchinson, or the BBC Radio for
Schools pamphlets) and to convince pupils that
success in reading is not determined by the quantity
to be read. The ideal of course is that pupils
should write their own plays, which make concessions
to the speaking voices of the group who will read

the parts.

The teacher, despite all that has gone before, will set the standard through the quality of his own reading and may need to exaggerate tone or accent if he is to indicate how important voice texture is in bringing a scene to life; a quick and suitably chosen burst of the Archers is usually enough to suggest this. He will also need to be prepared to demonstrate and ask pupils to demonstrate how they think certain words or lines need to be spoken, 'The stage direction says "sardonically". How do you think Edwin might say it?', 'The playwright hasn't given us any help here. Given what you know already, any suggestions as to how she might have said it?'. Reading parts aloud need not start with the complete play text; the teacher might well extract particularly vivid pieces of dialogue from pupils' own stories or plays and invite pairs to read them, simply to demonstrate how much can be contributed to the words on the page by performance, however informal. The teacher might ask the class to deduce as much as possible about the nature of the story from the extract and then compare this with the writer's own account of the story. No pupil should be made to read out his own work but there will be many who, while shy of reading it out themselves, will be happy to see it read by a capable colleague.

Pupils of all ages generally look favourably on the reading of plays, if only as a contrast to the reading that typically goes on in the English lesson. Approval is usually only withdrawn where the teacher has allocated parts poorly so that the least fluent readers are reading the more demanding parts, or where the play is inherently uninteresting or is being made so because the teacher is allowing fluent but undistinguished readers to destroy it in a monotone. Here drama adds to English the concept of conscious performance, which suggests that mere decoding is not enough, but that every drop of meaning must be extracted through the voice, since paralinguistic interpretation is denied, or at least for the time being. It is the equivalent to the theatrical read through, involving director and actors, which normally precedes any rehearsal of choreographed movement. In radio of course it is the performance. So those teachers and classes who aim less at a reading and more at an interpretation will approach the text carefully, using a sequence which moves closer and closer to the text. Let us assume that the teacher wishes to

introduce a one act play, for pleasure and as practice in using a wide range of reading voices, both
in the sense that it will allow a representative
range of pupils to take part and because it will
demand a variety in types of reading voices. Having
read and annotated the play in advance, the teacher
does not make the common mistake of assuming that
the pupils have an equivalent understanding of its
content and purpose, that is he will briefly explain
why he has introduced it at this point, what he hopes
it will disclose in the way of skills and understanding and he will give pupils ample time to read at
least the first part, silently. He may then ask
pupils to suggest the kind of play it is, what
actually happens and what it is about (type, plot
and themes). Alternatively, and with younger classes more sensibly, he will move on to focus on the
leading characters, 'What do you think each of them
actually looks like?' 'What do we know of them?'
'What sort of voices do you think they have?'. Such
discussion must precede the allocation of parts lest
only the actual readers feel they need contribute,
or retire to frantically read through their speeches.
The teacher might add to this an equally important
question, 'What's the point of asking ourselves
these questions?', hoping to make the point that
visualising the characters is important if they are
ever to emerge as anything like interesting three-
dimensional human beings (assuming that that is what
the playwright intended) and that, even where detailed stage descriptions are given, there is still room
for imaginative interpretation.

The best choice of play is one which allows the
division of the class into smaller groups where each
pupil has a meaningful part to play, if not always
to read. Pupils ideally have sufficient initiative
to allocate parts themselves, considering the suit-
ability of the voice for the part, rather than more
partisan criteria, but in the early days of the
teacher-class relationship this may be asking for
trouble and it may be more sensible for the teacher
to set the standard, working with the whole class,
at least initially. He has a choice between asking
for volunteers or playing the producer and nominat-
ing readers. There are obvious advantages and disadvantages to each: volunteers bring enthusiasm to
the part but only the more extrovert may volunteer
and in some classes, notably the senior ones, it is
considered infra dig to appear to court the teacher's
favour. In these cases it may be safer all round
to ask pupils to read parts, maintaining their

credibility with their peers and investing them with
the teacher's respect and trust that they can fulfil
the task. It is of course important that those who
do not volunteer or who are not chosen do not feel
left out, nor that they can safely doze off while
their colleagues are reading. They will play an
important part in discussing how certain lines are
said and in contributing to any final analysis. If
one reader is having difficulties with a part the
teacher may insert the 'understudy', or change
readers half way through the lesson. Once the reading has begun it should proceed as quickly as possible, since points of interpretation should have
been dealt with in advance. When the class's concentration span seems to be waning the teacher will
intervene to call a halt while the appetite to continue is still fairly healthy and before those who
are not actually reading become irrevocably restless.
This is 'performance' in one sense, but it can be
taken one stage further if one invaluable piece of
teaching equipment, the tape-recorder, is exploited
in order to create a more pressing need for 'getting
it right'.

Tape Recording
The tape-recorder, and for most of us that means the
cassette-recorder, can as this chapter will suggest,
become a valuable asset in English and drama work.
It fulfils several roles: it obviously records, thus
investing the ephemeral with a permanence and thus
an importance that it might not otherwise have.
Once the record is on tape it can be used as a
performance for others, perhaps other classes, even
other schools or local radio, and for future reference and as a teaching stimulus for subsequent work.
It can take the place and make a change from the
ubiquitous project folder, bringing together a wide
range of perhaps personally initiated work, a recorded anthology which frees the individual from the
tyranny of spelling mistakes and the red pen. For
most pupils the incentive to use the tape-recorder
will though be much more immediate: with few exceptions and surprisingly, given our sophisticated
technological age, pupils will listen with nervous
wonder to the sounds of their own voices, particularly when they have been required to adopt a tone or
accent which is not normally their own. Recording
suggests unequivocally what their voices are capable of and hints at the power of radio in inviting
its audience to use its imagination and, incidentally,
allowing the performers far more freedom in the

creation of special effects or the use of a cast of thousands. The tape recorder introduces the creative tension which is fired by the prospect of a 'real' performance; it has a disciplining effect since the cast will be required to get it right possibly for a single take. As a later chapter will suggest, its use offers a route into an analysis of radio's techniques, opportunities and limitations.

Any lively and interesting piece of reading can be taped and at best this will be pupils' own work, perhaps consciously written with recording in mind. Alternatively, there are a number of plays which, sometimes because they were written for the radio, invite recording. One such is Alan Ayckbourn's 'Ernie's Incredible Illucinations', 'a play for the classroom, where a boy's imaginings come to life', a one acter which is suitable for eleven to thirteen year olds. It contains at least eighteen speaking parts and only one character, Ernie, has anything approaching extended speeches. The cast list suggests the wide range of voice types : Ernie, Mum, Dad, Doctor, Receptionist, Officer, Auntie May, Referee, Timekeeper, Tramp, Barkers... and the fact that Ernie's imaginings take the characters into some vivid and bizarre situations invites exaggerated voices and sound effects. The latter can be managed without too much pre-planning, in the normal class-room : coughs, sneezes, the tramp of feet, crashes, screams, fairground noises, boos, cheers, a bell ringing, and the sound of howling wind, though at the very least teachers in nearby classrooms should be approached and warned. For those who feel that their pupils are not up to convincing imitations of the above, BBC sound effect recordings may help, but I have always found that part of the fun and the in-genuity comes from challenging 'the sound effect department', a distinct band of 'experts' to perfect their own versions, using the materials to hand. There are other plays in the 'Ernie' mould which lend themselves to classroom performance and recording, notably 'Five Green Bottles' by Roy Jenkins, 'Chicken' by Jon Rollason and 'The Whole Truth' by Ray Jenkins, suitable for eleven to fourteen year olds. These will be familiar to, and already tried and tested by those using BBC Radio for Schools pamphlets of the 1970s. They are now conveniently gathered in a single volume[2] and, given careful (but not exhaustive) preliminary reading, create excellent opportunities for recording and for animated discussion.

Recording should be firmly fixed to coherent objectives if it is not to lose its novelty and impetus and is not to be seen as a routine response to any play reading. The process of working towards a recording should not be hurried; if a recording is to take place at all the interpretation should be a careful one and each play, each scene will suggest the most sensible approaches to the performance. One example, considered in greater detail than is possible with the examples above, will perhaps reinforce these points:

Context

The class of thirty mixed ability third year (thirteen to fourteen year old) pupils have been focussing on the diary as a literary genre, beginning with their own experiences of keeping diaries, family diaries and class diaries. They have moved on to consider those of Anne Frank, Queen Victoria and Samuel Pepys among others. The last named has proved to be an unexpected success ('Who would have thought they were thinking like that then, Miss') and the teacher is happy to extend the theme to look at Pepys in the context of seventeenth century society and contemporary social events. Inevitably this has led into some research into the Great Plague (with the help of the history master, since the class are currently studying the Stuarts in their history lessons). The class, predictably, are fascinated by the fearsome and gruesome details of buboes, rats, death and decay and the teacher wishes to exploit this interest through some form of class recording which will bring them closer, she hopes, to a class realisation of the impact of the plague on one family. The teacher uses as stimulus 'Journal 1665'[3], a short play based on 'Journal of the Plague Year' by Daniel Defoe, which follows the effects of the plague through the streets of London from the summer of 1664 to December 1665 and contains extracts from the Diary of Samuel Pepys to add verisimilitude to the reconstruction.

The Lessons

The teacher arranges the classroom, in advance, so that six groups of five pupils are each seated around a central table. The groups are asked to read through the first four brief scenes of 'Journal 1665' silently, noting information which has added to what they already know of the Great Plague. This information is shared in a class discussion. The groups, working independently, then comment on the accompanying pictures, describing what they can glean from these illustrations alone. The teacher asks the groups to focus on the Prologue:

London. Summer. 1664. Narrow streets.
Cobbles. Old timbered houses, People. Many
poor. Shops. Horses, carriages, carts.
Noise! Rattle of wooden and iron wheels on
cobbles. Horses neighing. People calling
from the shops and streets.
Apprentices : What do you lack?
Hawkers : Lily-white vinegar. White-hearted
cabbages. Kitchen stuff.
Shopkeepers : Cherry Ripe. Peas. Strawberries.
Apples.
Milkmaids : (Rattling pails) Any milk wanted?
Hardware men : Have you any brass pots, iron
pots, skillets or frying pans to mend?
Mousetrap man : Buy a mousetrap, a mousetrap
or a tormentor for your fleas.
Fishwoman : Herring, cod, mackerel, oysters,
whiting.
(People quarrelling. Nobles arguing with poor
people).
Footman : Get out of his Lordship's way.
Drayman : I'll give his Lordship a piece of
my mind if he's not careful.
Whole streets swearing and shouting. Someone is
hurt. Pedestrians are splashed with mud; scream
with rage. Hanging pots outside a shop are
pulled down by somebody who runs by. Brawling
revellers. Terrible noise.
Smell! Disgusting. Dirty, filthy. Smells from
brewers, dyers, soap-boilers, refuse.
All rubbish thrown into street from the over-
handing upper stories of the timbered houses.
Bright clothes. People parading their finery.
Streets teem with people. Many backstreets,
narrow alleys and courtyards. Some gardens
with trees. Robbers.

The class are to concentrate on a careful re-read-
ing of this. One group is asked to read out its
version of the Prologue, with one pupil reading the
narrative. The teacher compliments them on their
reading and then, since it has been taped, plays
the recording back to the rest of the class with the
direction, 'Imagine that this forms part of a radio
broadcast. If you were director are there any suggestions you would immediately make as to how it could
be made even more interesting and convincing?'.
Several are proferred, 'We could do the sound effects
Miss', 'Make the voices all different so you could
tell when someone different is speaking', 'They
wouldn't get anyone to buy their stuff Miss, they're

not loud enough'. The groups are asked to take up
these suggestions and to note in rough the textures
of voices which will be used for each of the speaking parts, so that each is quite distinct in any
recording. When the groups have agreed this among
themselves they read the Prologue again. Already,
at least two of the groups are eagerly looking forward to the next scene, but the teacher feels that
the Prologue provides a sufficient basis for imaginative script work, which challenges pupils to
think and write for themselves. She suggests, 'So
far so good, but now let us look for the clues in
here that we might develop to produce our own London
street scenes set in the summer of 1664. For example, one single sentence, "People calling from the
shops and streets" makes you wonder what the people
are calling about. Any offers for topics of conversation?.. Yes, all possible. We could now
develop that little slice of life into a script
which might be suitable for recording. Any more
ideas?' Certain of the boys immediately focus on
'People quarrelling' and the rich, man poor man
confrontation. Other suggestions are, 'Street
cries', 'A street accident', 'Robbers!' and 'Someone important passes through'. The teacher has
anticipated these suggestions and has incorporated
them into a worksheet, where each group is directed
to one of the assignments:

A. With the help of the street cries in the
   Prologue, but without copying them, note
   down on the paper provided your own street
   cries. Decide:
   Who you are : Name, age, background, etc.
   What you are selling/offering.
   What your selling line will be e.g. the
   freshness, cheapness, etc. of your produce/
   service. Write it down (not more than four
   lines).
   Use the description at the beginning of the
   Prologue as an introduction to your own
   series of street cries. Experiment: try
   overlapping some of the voices, making some
   musical, altering the rise and fall of the
   cries.
B. Take as your theme 'The Arrival of
   the Plague '.
   Set the scene by using the first half of
   the Prologue.
   Add to this the sound of customers' comments
   as they respond to the sellers' cries.

41

Show and script what happens as the news slowly, and then more rapidly, filters through that someone in a nearby doorway has been struck down by the plague.

C. A seventeenth century 'reporter' describes the scene in a London street in the summer of 1664. As he is in the middle of his commentary he is interrupted by a call for help. An accident involving several people has occurred and he switches from commentator to interviewer of those involved and those who witnessed the proceedings.

D. Night time in Broadacre Street, in the heart of the city of London, summer 1665. The night watchman is making his rounds, ensuring that those who have come in close contact with the plague do not escape to the countryside. He hears moans from a doorway and when he goes to investigate finds himself approached by a group of children whose mother is already dead and whose father is dying. They appeal to him to let them flee, describing their pitiful existence. When this is unsuccessful they attempt to bribe him and then threaten him. The night watchman explains what will happen if he agrees.

E. 'King Charles Passes By':
Script your own scene in a London street market, summer 1664.
Show through the cries of the market tradesmen and the responses of their customers and the passers by, what is being bought and sold and current topics of conversation (the monarchy, the court, local gossip etc.). Show how those on the street gradually become aware that a grand carriage is trying to make its way through, that the carriage contains someone very important and finally that the V.I.P. is no less than Charles II himself. Make clear who accompanies him in the carriage, what he has stopped to see or buy and his subjects' reactions (both public - and private!).

F. 'A Traveller in Time':
Imagine and script the scene when a time-traveller from the 1980s attempts to interview a number of personalities from a London street in the summer of 1664 and is gradually drawn into commenting on their way of life, habits and opinions to an

        extent where the interviewer finds himself
        interviewed by those who have gathered
        around him.

G. A suggestion of your own, based however
        loosely on a hint from the Prologue,
        described in this space and agreed with
        your teacher.

These were of course only the bare bones of the assignments and pupils were encouraged to decide exactly how the scripts would come to be written themselves. Some groups produced a joint effort, while others produced two or more versions which were then judged by the group. The teacher was always happy to act as literary consultant and reference library, pointing pupils to appropriate reference works and acting as a sounding board for first drafts. She felt not the slightest twinge of compunction at linking English and drama work so closely with history, far from it, since she felt that the historical context provided a framework for those pupils who so often found it difficult to know what to write. When teacher and group were happy with the reading of the script, the group was invited to record this in the nearby house head's office, since he was away teaching at the time. The result was, when edited, a forty minute tape which class, English teacher and history teacher felt was sufficiently convincing, interesting and historically accurate to be used as a history teaching resource with other groups, and formed a launching off point for future improvisation, based on 'The Life and Times of Samuel Pepys'.

Working on a Small Canvas

The examples above suggest, however briefly, the interpretative scope accorded to pupils by even a short scene and heavily teacher-defined tasks. Pupils can feel very disconcerted when they are given too great a choice, too wide a theme; the work is spread thin and they are not forced to push hard at the circumference of the task, to exploit all its possibilities. While experienced groups, who have already learned to read the teacher's mind, may be able to respond intelligently and decisively co a wide brief, the inexperienced or inhibited pupil of any age will need secure guidelines if he is not to flounder among the wealth of options open to him. With younger classes enthusiasm and energy at least provide the momentum to get pupils on their feet and doing, but for older students launching into mime and movement of any sort may be ruled out by self-consciousness and tension. Such students will need gradual weaning into drama which takes them from teaching methods they know and trust to a point where they can get to their feet and improvise.

Script work offers a secure way in, and for those who feel that the language of the great playwrights of the past presents an insurmountable barrier to the less confident student, there are other, more modern writers who offer a similar challenge without the initial obscurity. Harold Pinter's plays, for example, abound in almost cyclical exchanges which ask their readers and actors to look behind, around and before the words in the script and to practise meanings by experimenting with the delivery:

> Davies Uuuuuuuuhhh! What! What! What!
> Uuuuuuuuhhh!
> (Mick lets him go, goes slowly to a
> chair, sits, and watches Davies,
> expressionless).
> (Silence)
> Mick   What's the game? (Silence) Well?
> Davies Nothing, nothing, nothing.
> (A drip sounds in the bucket overhead.
> They look up. Mick looks back to Davies)
> Mick   What's your name?
> Davies I don't know you. I don't know who you
> are. (Pause).
> Mick   Eh?
> Davies Jenkins.
> Mick   Jenkins?
> Davies Yes.
> Mick   Jen...kins. (Pause). You sleep here
> last night?
> Davies Yes.
> Mick   Sleep well?
> Davies Yes.
> Mick   I'm awfully glad. It's awfully nice to
> meet you. (Pause). What did you say
> your name was?
> Davies Jenkins! (Pause).
> Mick   Jen...kins.

There are questions that any reader must ask of these lines from 'The Caretaker'. These questions become more pertinent and pressing if performance is envisaged, and the nature of the questions will be determined by the interrogator: What will the actor playing Mick and the actor playing Davies ask of

their own lines and those of the other? What overall view may the director have of this scene? How
will it relate to the rest of the play? How will
the designer liaise with the director? What will
he ask of the script and decide are the implications
in terms of costumes, scenery and props? Before
pupils can produce their own actor's/director's/
designer's annotated script they will need to
develop the skills necessary to interrogate a text.
The expertise developed here will prove invaluable
in gauging the intentions and implications of any
piece of writing. Pupils will need to identify for
themselves the questions which this scene poses:
Is Mick's opening cry submissive/retaliatory/path-
etic...? Is Mick bemused/aggressive/defensive...
as he watches Davies, and thus is his next question
'What's the game?' invested with any special meaning? Does the drip in the bucket break a spell/
change the tone of the conversation/merely provide
an accompaniment...? How much is Davies giving
away if he discloses his name? What sort of word
is 'nice' as it is commonly used? How does Mick
speak it here? Are any particular gestures demanded
by the words? And most fundamental : Is there only
one right way of reading these words and lines? Are
there any wrong ways? Pupils can build up to such
deliberation by writing and reading out an interview
which on the page appears innocuous but which can be
interpreted in such a way that the interviewer responds to the interviewee's answers so as to under-
mine his confidence and even threaten his sense of
his own credibility and identity. Both the extract
from The Caretaker and this suggested preamble have
the advantage that they can be acted out with the
two protagonists seated for much of the time, fitting them for the conventional classroom and fixing
attention firmly on the words and their reverberations.

From Classroom to Open Space

The exercises described above suggest how much drama
work can effectively take place in the average
sized classroom, given a willingness to rearrange the
furniture. Some older and introverted students will
feel safer leaving it at that but the young, the
enthusiasts, bursting with ideas which need a greater stage would, in their own way, support the tenet
that 'At all stages it must be appreciated that the
spoken word cannot be realistically taught unless
there is scope for the bodily and paralinguistic
features on which all effective communication heav-

ily relies'.[4] Thus, greater space frees drama to
attempt almost anything, but such freedom can be
threatening unless it is hedged by rational restrictions and the transition from constricted classroom
to liberating space has to be carefully managed.
Older pupils, who have never done any drama, may
react to an open space, not by running wild, but in
an equally disconcerting way; their limbs may become tense and stiff, they may huddle in corners and
not unnaturally show a marked reluctance to risk
valued clothes (where school uniform is not worn)
on a dirty floor. It is important not to make the
fatal mistake of putting them into situations which
they will see as undignified or strange, thus 'I
want you to imagine that you are explorers strugg-
ling through the jungle', is likely to be greeted
with glum faces, passsive resistance or titters of
embarrassment. Better to start with something the
class know and trust, such as group discussion,
particularly discussion based upon a problem with a
realistic context and one which has a relevance for
their work in the classroom. Such a task will
legitimise sitting in groups, discussing options
and deciding on courses of action. The discussion
and the adoption of roles becomes the enactment,
'As chairman of this sub-committee I would like to
propose...' and pupils feel happier hidden behind
the veneer of an identity which is not their own.
Once the teacher has won the class's trust, convinced them that because the space is there they do
not have to risk peer group credibility with extravagant gestures and funny voices then the route towards mime and improvisation, in its fullest sense,
can be a gradual and supportive one.

NOTES

1. John Allen, Drama in Schools: Its Theory
and Practice (Heinemann, 1979).
2. Richard Hendry, Three Short Plays (Heinemann 1975).
3. See: William Martin and Gordon Vallins,
Routes (Evans, 1968).
4. H.M. Inspectorate, Curriculum 11-16, Working Papers (D.E.S., 1977).

Chapter Three

PUSHING OUT THE LANGUAGE FRONTIERS

'THE MINEFIELD'

Skill in using language comes through practice, and
particularly through confronting unfamiliar situations which test the individual's ability to
exploit and extend his existing language skills,
since 'All of us, to some extent, have a view of
language as a minefield when we have to use it in
unfamiliar circumstances'.[1] When we feel anxious
about such situations it is not because we lack the
basic linguistic resources to participate but because we are not sure which register to adopt to fit
the occasion, the topic and the personnel. A register is simply the language demanded by a particular context, perhaps that of the court, of the playground, board meeting, even bus stop or launderette.
Such milieux demand certain conformist language
types : to use the language of the football terraces
in a convent might produce comic or disastrous results, and, closer to home, the new pupil who add-
resses his head teacher as familiarly as his mate is
in for a rude shock. All pupils are aware, if only
subconsciously, of this minefield. Few are given
the opportunities in school to learn safe routes
through it. One of the most vital contributions of
drama to English and language work is in providing
a framework for the use of language in context:

> The use of drama as a teaching medium provides
> varied opportunities for children to use lang-
> uage in an exciting and experimental way, thus
> increasing vocabulary and developing an
> interest in oral communication otherwise scarc-
> ely touched upon in normal everyday teaching.[2]

THE 'VOICES' OF DRAMA

Teachers of English have tended in the past to have
a shaky grasp of the nature and development of language, and where the grasp has been firmer we have
tended not to share our knowledge with our pupils,
almost as though concepts like register, accent,
dialect and the notion of language categories were
slightly subversive in the classroom and hardly on a
par with the 'true' language work of the comprehension exercise, summary or slot-filling exercise.
Certain text books[3] have attempted to legitimise the
study of language acquisition and language use but
most of us have a long way to go if we are to convince our pupils of the versatility of the language
skills they already possess, let alone extending
these in the classroom. Each pupil needs to be
shown that he or she is not a single entity but that
each makes many, sometimes sophisticated, role shifts
in the course of the day and each of these shifts
will demand a new language use. Each pupil will have
his own idiolect, that is his own personal dialect,
but this splinters into many parts to adapt to those
whom he meets. Around the breakfast table he may be
contrite son, bossy older brother or patronising
grandchild, each with its own 'voice'. Each lesson,
each teacher, will come trailing a new part for the
pupil to play; different peer groups, different
friends will have different expectations, different
demands and this is just to put it at its simplest.
It is little wonder that so many pupils appear as
'Jekyll and Hyde' cases in their reports or in parents' evening discussions.
     Drama work can provide opportunities for pupils
to play out their own familiar roles and registers,
where they are encouraged to explore and analyse the
inevitable shifts in language and the paralinguistic
means of communication which accompany them. Drama
can go further in encouraging the exploration which
accompanies the taking on of unfamiliar voices, where
the pupil adopts the identity and perception of
another. Such exploration may be useful in preparing pupils for roles they may have to play in later
life, as employee, unemployed, parent, student,
beneficiary, supplicant, defendant... but it has a
more significant purpose in helping to develop the
openmindedness which accompanies tolerance and
intelligence. More specifically, it may lead to a
greater imaginative understanding of the opposite
sex, another generation, or other racial groups.
Such exploratory role play provides the creative

base matter for the many imaginative excursions that any story teller must make. Drama has the capacity for tuning the ear to the nuances of meaning by encouraging pupils to look behind and beyond the face value of words to grasp that, 'To understand another's speech, it is not sufficient to understand his words - we must also understand his thought. But even that is not enough - we must know his motivation'.[4]

The corollary of language use and language acquisition is listening, and training pupils to listen makes language development possible. To talk of training may seem far-fetched, after all listening is something we surely just do, and pupils do for well over half their 'communicating' time in schools.[5] But it is just because our pupils spend so much time listening, usually to a single speaker, their teacher, and because we have traditionally been rather casually neglectful of its importance in the classroom that we need to be more aware of tasks that stimulate active and engaged listening. We need to bring our pupils' attention to what they might listen for, why, and how,

> We feel that the motivating force of interesting language, produced not by far-distant literary figures but by people in the world around us, engaged in living and communicating as we do, is a great stimulus to the development of listening ability. We also feel that a knowledge of some of the features of language and how language operates is likely to be useful in this connection. To put it another way we do not conceive of 'listening skill' as something existing in the abstract, unrelated to such matters as the interest of the material, or the knowledge of the listener - indeed to the whole context.[6]

Drama provides just those whole contexts in which interesting language takes root.

There are certain types of language which are most likely to be neglected in English lessons where drama does not play a part; these are, language which justifies, criticises, commends, monitors, directs, reflects, questions, draws comparisons, decides, infers, persuades, projects, negotiates and manipulates. Or, to put it another way, it is the teacher and not the pupils who is using these. What general drama strategies encourage the practice of these language types?

Co-operation: Asking pupils to work as a pair
or in a group where they are responsible for
as much of the decision-making as possible
encourages language which directs and negotiates, anticipates and persuades.

Planning: Allowing pupils ample time to think
about what they are about to take on encourages language which predicts and projects.

Evaluation: Allowing pupils opportunities to
interpret and assess their own work and that of
others encourages language which justifies,
criticises (in the best sense), commends,
persuades, compares, questions and infers.

What this attempts to suggest is that the doing,
the improvisation, the acting out, accounts for
only a part of the language output. The planning
talk, the directing talk, the questioning and the
assessment are what make any sort of progress possible.

LANGUAGE PRACTICE

We might profitably begin, like the teachers in the
accounts which follow, by exploring the links between language and stereotypes:

Exploring and Exploding Stereotypes
This class of fourth year pupils have been reading
Keith Waterhouse's novel 'Billy Liar' and have noted
the many voices Billy uses, when with his mother,
father, gran, his contemporaries at work, and with
his girlfriends. The teacher wishes to demonstrate
that Billy is not alone in meeting and using different registers but that everyone who wishes to
preserve relationships with a range of people is
bound to adopt a different voice for each one, to a
greater or lesser extent. In order to make the
work easier, less potentially embarrassing for the
class, the teacher asks them to focus on fictional
but familiar characters:
   (A) is a prisoner on remand for assaulting an
old lady and stealing from her. In the course of
a month in the remand centre he (she) will be allowed visits from a number of those most concerned
about his (her) welfare. The class suggests that
these might include his mother, wife, son, a religious representative whether vicar, priest, rabbi or
imam, his friend and his boss. Each visitor in turn

faces the accused across a table and shows by what
they say and how they say it, the nature of their
concerns and their relationship. A 'screw' inter-
venes formally to close each interview and at the
end of the series of visits he demonstrates the
nature of his relationship with the accused as he
leads him back to his room.

The class do not go into this work blind but
are fed, and discuss, information concerning the
prison service and criminal justice system. The
pupils develop and share their work. After seeing
a few examples certain stereotypes emerge: the fussy
and protective mother; the bullet-headed, harsh
screw; the effete middle class, patronising vicar;
the hard-drinking, irresponsible mate. This leads
class and teacher into a discussion about the
nature of stereotypes: Where do they come from?
How are they reinforced? How likely are they to
give a true picture? To what extent are they justified by the pupils' own dealings and relationships
with such people? The class, split into groups,
return to their work, not to reject stereotypes
outright, since they have decided that they are true
in part, but to show that beneath the veneer the
characters are altogether more complex, perhaps
more defensive and unsure of their roles, in this
strange game. To help this process along the teacher
suggests that each speaker is given one area of guilt.
The class suggest that the remand prisoner's wife
may be having an affair with his mate, the prison
officer may be facing disciplinary charges, the vicar may feel impotent in the face of the wickedness
around him and the prisoner, while pretending his
innocence, is actually guilty as charged. The groups
are asked to show how each speaker attempts to dis-
tract attention, sometimes crudely, sometimes subtly, away from these areas. The groups are finally
asked to choose any one character and to place them
in a situation which reveals other facets of their
personalities and use of language.

In the second example, a class of thirteen
year old pupils have been, with the aid of 'Web of
Language',[7] focussing on idioms, cliches and thence
'small talk'. They have experimented with short
scripts which suggest the cosy, familiar feel of
small talk devices which help to establish and
re-establish relationships and have been asked to
write their own equivalents, which they might use
in the course of the day when meeting a friend. Each
pupil has next produced his own list of idioms and
cliches with some help from those at home, since

they have been asked to note particularly those most favoured by their friends and family. The class has enjoyed developing a conversation containing a string of cliches and idioms. The teacher next divides the class into groups and presents each pupil with a role play card which will decide their identities. The scene is set in a small sub-post-office; all the customers are pensioners meeting, as it happens, for the first time. Each card indicates a name and two or three distinguishing features or interests. For example:

> Albert Petherbridge : age 72 : married : has trouble with his kidneys, otherwise healthy : grows prize marrows.

The class are asked to add any other distinguishing features for themselves, before joining the queue formed from the members of the group. One pupil plays the part of the sub-postmaster (mistress). To ease the pupils into the situation, the teacher builds in a 'disturbance' : the sub-postmaster is in a bad mood and takes his bad temper out on the first customer, who mumbles his words. This causes ripples back through the queue which bring the pensioners closer together and into conversation. Each group discusses its work; the teacher asks them to consider whether any unexpected facets of character have been revealed by the disturbance : Have they all reacted differently? Has a leader emerged? Will any more meaningful relationships be formed because of this group experience? This leads into a class discussion about the stereotypes associated with older people, their interests and the language they use. The teacher asks them to think about the impression conveyed by the media and particularly television. He asks pupils to describe to the rest of their group an old person they know well, in as much detail as possible but without naming names. The group is asked to decide whether these descriptions reinforce or demolish any stereotypes.

Registers
This teacher wishes to alert her class of third year pupils to the range of registers around them. She begins by playing them a tape-recording and asks them to identify the kind of person talking. She has compiled the tape from radio and television news magazine programmes and the extracts include a militant trade unionist, a religious affairs correspondent, an eloquent and persuasive politician,

an admiral of the fleet, a weather forecaster, a
news reader, a demonstrator interviewed on the
pavement and a gentleman who specialises in keeping
ferrets down his trousers. The class are asked to
note the characteristics of the content, type and
tone of voice and any other distinguishing features.
They are also asked to decide how important the tone
or tones of voice were in suggesting who was speaking and about what. Having shared their findings,
the teacher asks, 'How much can the voice of someone
tell you about that person?' The class pool their
ideas : class, age, sex, mood, job sometimes, intelligence sometimes. The teacher asks, 'Do you think
the people we have heard always talk like this?'
The class is undecided. She asks them to think of a
situation in which it would be inappropriate for the
speaker to talk in the way he or she has done on the
tape, and to develop this idea in pairs. Several
situations emerge : the admiral talking to his young
grandson, the weather forecaster who is asked by a
bus conductor 'Nice weather i'n' it?', the politician in the dentist's chair, the trade unionist trying to evict his (her) daughter from the bathroom.
The teacher introduces the idea of 'registers' suited to different situations and asks pupils to make
a list which suggests the register of school. She
helps them by reading out Simon Croft's poem 'I'm
a Reasonable Man' which begins:

It will be your time you'll be wasting after
                                        school.
I'll treat you like babies if you act the fool.

Having made their lists, pupils are given the option
of transforming it into a poem and reading it aloud,
or performing the list as convincingly as possible in
front of the 'recalcitrant' class. The effect is
often comic as pupils, sometimes unconsciously,
adopt the accompanying gestures of recognisable
members of staff.

The teacher asks the class to suggest other
registers with which they are familiar, for example,
the registers of the football terrace, changing room,
the riding school, the hospital, the surgery, the
disco and church. In order to challenge their inventiveness, the teacher gives each pair of pupils
a card which has a single line, characteristic of
one or more registers, on it:

So it's the big end that's gone has it?
Now what seems to be the matter with your back?

53

Pushing Out The Language Frontiers

      Call Lesley Jones...
      Take your elbows off the table...
      Didn't diddums want to join in then?
      Calling AK 34...Come in AK 34...
      You know the grievance procedure, Smith...
      Three pints, two chocos and two raspberry yogs
                                please.
      Pass the mole wrench, Bert...
      Down the path he went, hoppity, hoppity...

Pupils are asked to use their line as a handle into
a short piece of improvisation which develops the
relationship suggested by the card. Pupils are then
asked to devise their own 'register lines'. The
teacher then asks them deliberately to mismatch the
lines, cutting through stereotypes with comic effect.
She suggests examples: A car crazy doctor asking,
'So it's the big end that's gone is it?', conduct-
ing the surgery consultation as though the patient
is a fast car; an officious female prime minister
telling a senior cabinet minister to 'Take your
elbows off the table, Willie...'; a parliamentary
correspondent who has spent too much time in the
members' bar reporting on the day's dealings in
parliament with the words, 'Down the path he went
hoppity, hoppity...' and a keeper at the London Zoo
declaring to a squawking parakeet, 'You know the
grievance procedure, Smith...'. The class consider
familiar comedians and comedy programmes and analyse
the extent to which they use this device in order to
win laughs.

Opening Doors
This class of twelve year old pupils have been
studying synonyms. They have offered their own for
such basic words as man - woman - big - small - good
- bad and have selected certain synonyms which imply
localised contexts before comparing their own lists
with those in Roget's Thesaurus. Under 'Adj. bad'
they are intrigued to find a selection which includes
the following: arrant, vile, base, gross, black, as
bad as bad can be, wretched, measly, low-grade,
execrable, awful, shoddy, ropy, punk, faulty, in-
competent, foul, rotten, septic, vicious, accursed,
heinous, deplorable, beastly, revolting, diabolical.
This prompts a great deal of discussion concerning
the shades of difference in meaning in these words
and the teacher asks for suggestions from the list
which imply specific contexts. The class, working
in pairs or groups of three or four, use a single
choice of word as a starting point, a trigger for

their drama work. For example:

> Two old ladies, for whom 'punk' is a four
> letter word, witness a youth with orange
> spiky hair talking to his girlfriend in a
> part of the park they consider their own.

> A knight is challenged by an authoritarian
> overlord to make amends for his 'heinous'
> crime.

> A rather fastidious aristocratic lady complains
> about the 'beastly' creature she has found
> in her food.

This last example leads into a survey of euphemisms,
colloquialisms and slang, and ways of getting an
audience to do something to order. The pupils compile lists of ways of conveying the same imperative
from suble nod, through curt gesture to:

> Sit! (Please)
> Sit down
> Take a seat
> Have a seat
> Would you like a seat?
> Rest your weary bones
> Have a pew
> There's a seat
> Be seated
> Here's a seat
> Take the weight off your feet
> Draw up a chair
> Do sit down
> I think we have a chair for you somewhere
> For goodness sake sit down
> Would you mind sitting down?
> Sit down, there's a good fellow

The pupils practise the ways these might be said
in order to reflect different relationships and
intentions. They are then asked to explore the
nature of this relationship, incorporating the
imperative or invitation at some point in their
improvisation.
     The class have, in the mean time, been reading
C.S. Lewis's 'The Lion, the Witch and the Wardrobe'
and Lucy's entry into a mysterious world via the
wardrobe door prompts a look at what doors may lead
into and on to. The class start by producing a
display, with the help of their art teacher, featur-

ing all the doors they can think of, portrayed as a
frieze and labelled and described underneath. The
frieze includes the doors of: Number Ten, a prison
cell, a rocket capsule, a secret tunnel, a haunted
house, the doors in 'Alice in Wonderland' and
'Through the Looking Glass', a church door, a door
in a tree, doors in nursery rhymes, the door to the
land of 'earthly delights'...The teacher suggests
that, as important as the door itself is what or who
lies behind it. First the cliches are exhausted:
the ghost, prime minister, the prisoner, but then
each pupil is asked to nominate something or someone
unexpected hiding behind the door each has chosen to
portray on the frieze, so that anyone knocking on the
door would be thrown off balance. These are then
added to the frieze during an art lesson. The pupils
are asked to develop this meeting dramatically with
the help of a partner, where appropriate. The teacher then asks, 'But what if it is not the knocker at
the door who meets the unexpected, but the person
who opens the door?'. She asks the pupils, working
in groups of four, to discuss the nature of the unexpected. Predictably they offer, a pools win, the
return of a long lost relative, an angry neighbour,
a criminal. The teacher encourages them to stretch
their imagination further: an animal, a traveller
from another time or planet, a mirror image, a new
view, a huge and mysterious parcel, the postman with
a very strange letter...Those who will open the door,
from each pair of pupils, will do so unaware of what
lies behind it; the 'visitor' will have the initiative and the 'resident' will have to assimilate and
react to whatever is said or happens when the door
is opened. Both residents and visitors are asked to
prepare their roles carefully and independently, to
consider how they move, speak, feel and the impression they are going to make on the other. The teacher
hopes that, unprepared for how the other will react,
each will be surprised into the sort of dynamic use
of language which is sometimes ruled out by the
self-conscious planning ahead of drama work.

'Metamorphosis'
This English teacher, in the course of a month's
drama work, wishes to give his able third year pupils more practical experience of identifying and
using a range of language types, and particularly
that language which seeks to persuade, manipulate,
project and justify. He also wants to put his pupils
into positions where they have problems to solve.
The class have been discussing how they would react

if something totally unexpected were to happen in
their families and the teacher wishes to explore how
the stress of such an upheaval would affect individual members of the family and their use of language. Without mentioning Kafka's 'Metamorphosis',
he feeds the pupils a narrative framework which
approximates to that in the short story:

Characters	Father, mother, son and daughter. The son is in his early twenties, the daughter in her late teens; both are unmarried and live with their parents. Brother and sister have always been closer to each other than to their parents. Grandparent, cleaning lady (comes in three mornings a week), son's boss (who takes a keen interest in the progress of one of his most promising employees).
Situation	The son is the major bread-winner; his father is unemployed and even if his wife were not often ill, would not approve of her seeking a job. The daughter works for half the week as part of a job-sharing scheme.
The Unexpected	One morning the son awakes to find that he is a giant insect. He can think rationally but the sounds he makes are not human and his family do not realise that he can understand them perfectly well.

The class, divided into groups of six or seven, are
asked first to fill out this framework, to decide
details of age, personal characteristics and opinions, to build up a picture of the home in which the
family lives and of their relationships. They are
asked to identify possible areas of strain present
before the metamorphosis (the father's unemployment,
the restriction of the wife's freedom to work, the
presence of a grandparent). These factors emerge
from the discussion groups, each of which has its
own 'scribe', and the resulting notes form the basis
for the ensuing drama work.

The groups are asked to focus, not on the son-
insect's feelings, but on those of the rest of the
family and particularly how each is likely, given

all they now know about them, to discover their
son's strange metamorphosis. The groups are asked
to act this out, at first just imagining the insect
and then incorporating someone playing the part, to
gauge which seems the more successful. Having explored these moments of discovery within the family,
the groups are asked to introduce interested parties from the outside world, the cleaning lady and
the boss, to explore the effect of their appearance
on the family's relationships with each other and
with the son.

In the next stage of their work, the groups
identify and consider the series of problems which
now confront the family, which must include: finding alternative means of financial support, deciding
whether the insect should be allowed to live or not,
if not the implications of killing him, if so the
problem of caring for him-it adequately, deciding
the extent to which he constitutes a health risk
and the extent to which they can afford to allow
their problems to become known. They must decide
whether they should treat him as a much-loved son
who is temporarily deranged or as a grotesquely
huge insect which has destroyed their son and now
threatens the whole family. They must confront the
deeper more philosophical questions, 'Why should we
be picked on in this way?', 'Have we been guilty of
some offence which has merited this horrific punishment?'. The groups soon come to realise that an
apparent solution for any one of these problems
brings in its wake a fresh progeny of problems. The
best that can be hoped for is a fairly rational compromise which seeks to control, however temporarily,
an irrational problem. The groups are then asked to
make each member of the family a mouthpiece for a
different point of view, to be expressed in a family conference which will be acted out. Each member of the family will be called upon to justify his
or her opinions and to anticipate the likely consequences of their proposals, and to suggest something of the inner strains in the family's relationships which complicate decision making.

The class next imagine the scene in the family
home a fortnight on: Is the insect-son still alive?
If so, what is his relationship with those who meet
him? If not, how did his death come about? How do
the family react to their 'bereavement'? How successfully are the family coping with the other problems identified earlier? One group opts to demonstrate the inevitable changes, however minor, which
have taken place, in a scene which is acted out.

Other groups opt to explore what happens when 'The news is out'. In one scene a nosey neighbour talks her way into the insect's room; in another the cleaning lady, who has been dismissed, is quick to exploit the bizarre story and sells her tale to a tabloid newspaper. As an associated written task, pupils are asked to demonstrate how the story might feature in a tabloid and a 'serious' daily newspaper. Finally, the story is taken up by a nation-wide television news programme which interviews the whole family, in turn, in their own home. The groups explore the extent to which the stated reactions and opinions on the air coincide with the speakers' behaviour when the cameras are not present. One group returns to the initial 'discovery' scenes to look at them from the point of view of the insect-son who only has limited means for making his feelings known and soon discovers that any sudden gesture can have a cataclysmic effect on his audience. The group presents the spoken thoughts of the insect-son as he makes his own discovery of the sometimes well-meaning, often cruel behaviour of those he looks to for protection.

The teacher points out that this completed sequence of English and drama work could form the basis for a play, short story, series of monologues or transcription and leaves this as a classwork or homework option for the class. He finally reads the class 'Metamorphosis' and thus provides an interesting opportunity for the groups to compare their own elaboration of the framework with that of Kafka. It also challenges them to decide whether the characters, their own or Kafka's, would have reacted in this way.

Skills in Argument

Most of us can easily identify when we disagree with something but do not always find it easy to hit upon the arguments which will articulate our opposition. We are like the animals in George Orwell's 'Animal Farm' who know that they are dismayed by Napoleon's expulsion of Snowball, realise the enormity of the changes around them and 'would have protested if they could have found the right arguments'. The skills demanded in the debating chamber, in committee, in an interview or in the school council meeting come with practice and can be fostered in the English classroom. It is a mistake to think that the skilful presentation of such arguments largely depends on scrupulous research. True, this is undeniably a help, but more important is the confi-

dence to select a few key points, to see the wood
for the trees and to push home an advantage. Drama
provides a context for such skills, a context which
makes the outcome more meaningful, where arguments
do not exist in a classroom vacuum but are the products of the feelings of recognisable and fallible human beings.

The account which follows describes how one
teacher of English attempted to develop such skills
by placing her class of fourteen year old pupils in
both familiar and unfamiliar situations which call
for skills in presenting a particular argument or
point of view.

The teacher presents the class with the following
description of a family: Father and mother, two
teenage children and a grandparent. The latter has
been living with the family ever since the death of
his or her spouse but is becoming increasingly difficult to care for. The mother, who is inevitably
carrying much of the burden, feels that she will
have to sacrifice her part-time job if the situation
does not change, since the family do not qualify for
special help. The class, split into groups of five,
are given this description without preamble and are
asked to consider the question which it raises but
does not answer. For example: What is the nature of
the grandparent's disability? Whose mother or father is he, she? How sound is the relationship between husband and wife? To what extent does the
grandparent impinge on the life of each member of
the family? Having decided on such questions and
answered them for themselves, the groups prepare and
act out a scene which looks at the situation from
the point of view of one of the members of the family. Thus each group specialises in one view point.
The teacher invites the class to see their colleagues interpretations and to notice the different
angles which each portrays. The teacher hopes that
these scenes will provide each character with sufficient impassioned arguments to present to the rest
of the family at the 'summit meeting', when the
mother shocks the family into making some sort of
decision about the grandparent's future. She next
asks the pupils, still working in their groups, to
produce as detailed a profile as possible of each of
the characters, looking particularly at their aspi-
rations, interests, anxieties and relationships with
the rest of the family. All this prepares for the
final scene when the family confront the issue.
This is acted out and the class-audience is asked to
comment on the relative effectiveness of the argu-

ments they have heard and the techniques used by
these individuals to get their points across.
    The class identify the following techniques:
The use of 'hard' facts and the reference to external 'truths' (It is well known that...'); the
use of flattery; dependence on status in the family,
pulling rank ('As the one who earns the money...'
'As the one who has to look after him...'); calling
on religion, ethics, morals as support ('It's totally unchristian to treat an old man in this way');
dependence on precedent ('If we do this we'll be the
first in our family to...'); using comparisons, particularly with other respected figures ('You would-
n't see X being so silly...'); calling on personal
experience ('I know exactly what'll happen...');
deferring decision-making to another when one knows
that their answer will support one's own ('Well
let's see what he thinks...'); rationally anticipating the results of the suggested and opposing course
of action ('Let's just see what'll happen if we do
as you suggest'); anticipating objections and spik-
ing them by getting in first (No doubt you're going
to object that...but that's nonsense...'). Pupils
are asked to identify which techniques were used
most effectively and powerfully in the scene and
to try to decide why this should be so.
    The teacher wishes to demonstrate that there
are not necessarily good and bad arguments but that
much of the skill depends on weighing up the nature
of the audience and anticipating which arguments will
be most influential in convincing them. She gives
the class an example: meeting the representatives of
certain distinct shareholder groups, prior to a crucial shareholders' meeting, in an attempt to persuade them to forgo dividends in the interests of
the company. The teacher asks pupils to suggest
other situations where it would be necessary to use
different arguments to fit different audiences. For
example:

    The car salesman attempts to sell the same car
    to a number of different potential buyers: the
    firm's representative, the middle-aged lady
    teacher, the teenage 'speed merchant'. The
    teacher brings the class's attention to the
    requirements of each buyer and the kinds of
    questions they must ask of the salesman in order
    to elicit the information they want.

    The doctor's waiting room 'revolt': the recep-
    tionist attempts to convince those who threaten

rebellion that it is worth their while to continue waiting.

'Please will you sponsor our bed push for
charity?': the participant goes from door to
door. The teacher brings the class's attention
to the two factors here, the principle of spon-
soring any event and the question of the particular charity which has been chosen.

The class decide on the information they will need
in order to bolster the acting out of their chosen
scenes and use some class time to discover a little
more about the background to each.

The teacher next invites the class to go well
beyond the pale of the familiar, at first back in
time. She asks the class to suggest moments in history where skill in argument must have played a
crucial role. By pooling their ideas the pupils
produce a long list which includes:

Lady Godiva attempting to convince her husband,
Earl Leofric, of the vital importance of lift-
ing the burden of taxes from the populace.

Sir Thomas More's wife attempting to convince
her husband that to die for the sake of a principle and his conscience is sheer folly.

Thomas Cromwell convincing Henry VIII that he
should marry Anne of Cleves

A mill hand convincing his down-trodden colleagues in a nineteenth century cotton mill in
Lancashire that they must down tools if they
are ever to gain better working conditions.

Space chiefs convincing the Congress of the
U.S.A. that the investment of billions of
dollars in a space programme, leading to the
first landing on the moon, is a worthy one.

Having gathered the necessary background information, with the help of the history department,
groups of pupils choose to develop a number of
different scenes. These lead into a look into the
future in order to anticipate those debates which
may seem fanciful now but could well be commonplace
by the end of the century. Pupils suggest:

The necessity for genetic engineering in general and cloning in particular.

The need to move populations in order to make better use of the earth's land mass.

The necessity for positive discrimination for the over sixties.

The need to teach certain types of pupils, for example the brightest, in separate establishments.

The pupils are asked to gear their arguments to a specified audience which will be played by the rest of the class, who will be permitted to present their objections from the floor. Thus, the Professor of Genetics might confront the 'Right to Free Life' campaigners. The teacher feels that taking on a particular role, whether scientist, salesman, mill hand or politician, provides the support and safeguard that many pupils need as a defence, so that, should their arguments fail, the failure is less their own than that of another into whose shoes they have stepped. Simultaneously, role play of this kind offers an imaginative focus which forces pupils to look at the life styles and concerns of others, to make the imaginative leap.

When the class feel more confident about marshalling and projecting their arguments the teacher challenges them to take on the apparently impossible and indefensible argument and, with some help from Stephen Pile's 'The Book of Heroic Failures', makes the point that ordinary human beings, as well as politicians, do try to convince themselves and each other that black is white and vice versa. She sets the situation up by teaching a classroom lesson which aims to test the class's attention, perception and ability to see through falacious arguments. This is made more difficult of course because the class's ears are becoming more attuned to the hollow or over elaborated sound of the meretricious case, but she at least wishes to make the point that the medium can be the message, particularly where a normally respected authority figure is presenting a point of view in apparently rational terms.

The teacher introduces a new theme for their work: they will look at the question of 'Intelligence'. The class reads a passage, purportedly written by an esteemed authority and extracted from an academic journal, which confirms, with the help of a number of non sequiturs and a distorted graph,

that 'Boys are inherently more intelligent than
girls'. There follows a short talk from the
teacher, annotating and supporting the passage and
making much use of the 'Of course it is well known
...' device in an attempt to carry pupils on the
crest of a majority view. The teacher introduces a
leader column, apparently from a 'respectable' newspaper, which comments on statistics which show that
boys do better at examinations than girls. She cir-
culates questionnaires at the end of the lesson to
'test how much you have remembered'. She then
informally tests pupils' recognition of the techniques which have been used to try to bombard them
into belief.
    In the next lesson, the teacher asks for sug-
gestions of debating proposals which should challenge all the class's dialectical skills. For
example,

    This house believes that:

    The keeping of pets should be made illegal.

    The population should be informed by official
    letter whom they are (consanguinity apart)
    allowed to marry.

    Private motorists should only be allowed to
    drive at weekends.

    People should be licensed to take baths or
    showers.

    Every alternate day pupils should be allowed to
    teach their teachers.

The class is divided into groups of five or six;
each group is asked to discuss and note down the
arguments for, and then against, their chosen proposal. They then choose a realistic context for the
debate and allot each other roles and personalities;
three will argue for the proposal and three against.
The allocation of roles and personalities is necessary if pupils are to be able to use all the weapons
of argument, at times citing the behaviour of each
other in order to push their points home. Before
attempting their own debate, pupils listen to part
of a particularly contentious session of 'Yesterday
in Parliament' and to 'You the Jury' (both Radio
Four), noting the tactics used in each.

FROM ROLE PLAY TO GROUP SIMULATION

Almost all of the above English and drama assignments involve role play of one sort or another.
Role play lies at the heart of drama and is one of
the central imaginative concerns of the writer of
fiction, and of the child at play. The idea of
pretending to be another comes easily to most children, less simple is the selection and adoption of
an appropriate register to convey to an audience
what the role taker intends. The egocentricity of
the speech of younger children should gradually
accommodate a recognition of the needs and concerns
of the listener, but pupils will need to be eased
into a realisation that they, as speakers, will not
only have to consider the audience but will need to
consider the possible role options open to them in
the course of conversation. That is, they will listen with not one but many ears, as they will speak
with not one but many voices.

In the 'real world' beyond the classroom, family and friendship roles are usually recognised and
familiar, taken as read. They come complete with a
context. In the classroom, role taking and making
can appear meaningless and trivial if they are not
placed in a setting which makes explicit their interest and relevance for the pupils. Simulation
packs[9] which describe an issue and then ask pupils
to adopt viewpoints and present arguments to defend
their case, provide useful starting points, in that
they accustom pupils to a way of working which involves group co-operation and decision making. But
commercially produced simulations have certain limitations for the teacher of English and drama, not
the least of which is their expense. More significantly, they cut out stages in the development of
roles, thus pupils only arrive at the scene at a
relatively late stage, as actors. Almost all the
ground work, the collecting of information, which
would be a necessary preliminary in real life, has
been done for them. Indeed, many actors work hard
to build, through their own research, an identifiable and accurate background for the character they
are about to play. It is far more satisfying and
valuable to build a class simulation from scratch
in the classroom and library, based on issues which
hold some immediate interest for those involved.
There is a set procedure which holds good for all
English and drama simulations:

1. The selection of an appropriate topic or

      issue and the identification of the part-
      icipants.
2.   The initial gathering and sharing of infor-
      mation.
3.   The allocation of roles and the identifi-
      cation of tasks.
4.   The enactment of the scene.

Selecting a Topic - Identifying the Participants

The teacher should not have to impose a topic but
should explain the sort of topic which is appropriate. It is one which is generally interesting to
all pupils, and complex in the sense that different
groups in the community (whether town, village,
school, hospital, club or road) will be able to present credibly different views about it. The teacher
might give a lead with a fairly humdrum example:
the use of land which has been seen as a recreation-
al amenity in order to build a multi-storey car park
He might then add that this is not immediately the
most interesting issue at hand and pupils should be
able to make their own suggestions and identify the
interested parties. One or more selections can then
be made:

    The local second division football club faces
    liquidation. A receiver is brought in to
    assess the club's viability. He suggests that
    the club may have a future if private investors
    and the local council are prepared to sink a
    large amount of private and public money into
    it. Interested parties: Directors - players -
    supporters' club - councillors - local resid-
    ents - rate payers' association.

    The local community relations council in a
    multi-racial sector of a large town has been
    shocked by the racist attacks on some of its
    members. Up to this point its protestations
    to the police and to the council have been
    muted and written, but now it has been stung
    into deciding to take to the streets to make
    its anger clear. The decision coincides with
    the news that a member of the royal family will
    be visiting the town on the projected day for
    the march. While the police cannot stop the
    march, they have asked the community relations
    council to postpone it until after the visit
    but they decide to make plans to go ahead re-
    gardless. Interested parties: The community
    relations council - police - chamber of

commerce - town council - relations of the
victims of attack - local residents' association.

The local education committee is considering
abolishing school dinners in a pilot school,
sacking the dinner ladies and altering the
school day from nine to three forty five, to
eight thirty to two o'clock, with one fifteen
minute break at eleven and no school dinner.
Interested parties: The education committee -
chief education officer and assistants - teaching staff - dinner ladies - parents - pupils.

These are deliberately challenging and controversial topics which are suited to more mature students. This does not of course mean that thought
provoking role simulation exercises are impossible
with less able and experienced groups. An expansion of the sort of subjects which are often used
as rather dreary essay titles. 'What I would do
with a thousand pounds, and why', 'Children should
be seen and not heard. Discuss' suggests possible
starting points:

A youth club has been left a thousand pounds
by a benefactor, to spend on one or more items
that it feels it needs. The youth club leader,
aware that all the club's basic requirements
have been met (i.e. furniture, refreshments,
television, cloakrooms, a games room and a
record player) and that the club is well heated,
decorated and staffed, asks interested parties
to suggest and justify ways of spending the
money. Interested parties: Club members - parents - youth club staff.

The teaching staff who organise and supervise a
Friday night disco which is held in school pre-
mises have decided to propose lowering the age
of admission from fifteen to thirteen. The
disco has always been popular and trouble free
in the past though recently there has been a
slight decrease in the number attending. The
head teacher, who must take ultimate responsibility, calls a meeting so that interested parties can declare their views. Interested parties: The over fifteen lobby - the over thirteen lobby - parents - organising staff.

The prime minister is considering appointing a

Minister for Children's Affairs to represent
the interests of those aged up to sixteen,
in parliament and the country at large. He
has called a meeting at which interested parties will be able to present their views and,
where they agree with the proposal in principle,
to define the minister's powers. Interested
parties: The under ten lobby - the ten to sixteen lobby - parents - teachers - social workers.

Gathering and Sharing Information

The teacher will need to settle on a choice of topic
well before the process begins in the classroom, in
order to decide on how the background information is
to be gathered. It may help to choose a topic from
the pupils' suggestions for which help is readily
at hand. It may well be that a member of the gov-
ernors or parent-teachers association is a councill-
or, social worker or industrialist and will be prepared to explain how his or her organisation works
and would go about confronting a contentious issue.
The gathering of information should not be seen as
merely a prelude to the more important role play and
debate which is to follow, for it is in this 'research' stage that much important learning will take
place. Pupils should come away from the role simulation exercise not only more practised in select-
ing and presenting arguments, but having gained
greatly in vicarious experience and knowledge of how
decisions are arrived at in a democratic society.
This is not to say that they will not be disillusioned. They may learn, for example, that the more
forceful speaker may be able to carry the day with a
less shrewd audience on the power of his rhetoric
alone. They may come to understand how it is that
speakers come to propose a course of action for
reasons quite other than those altruistic ones
stated.

Allocating Roles - Identifying Tasks

Having helped pupils to gather and share general
information concerning the simulation area, the
teacher will need to allocate roles, dividing pupils
into separate groups which will each speak as one of
the interested parties. By this stage each group
should have amassed a body of general information
which includes role descriptions for all those involved. As specific interested parties, they will
now need to probe the original outline for the significant facts which are omitted and to ask questions,

perhaps about the relationships between the parties,
'Have the police and the community relations council
seen eye to eye in the past?', 'Have the football
team attracted large crowds in the past?'. If this
part of the process is not to become endlessly pro-
tracted the teacher will need to have anticipated
the most telling questions and to have prepared
answers in advance which can be duplicated and distributed to pupils once they have thought hard about
these questions themselves. For example:

> You are THE SCHOOL DINNER LADIES
> You know you are slightly overstaffed and the
> decision to consider abolishing the school din-
> ner service in your school has not come as a
> great surprise. Nevertheless, you are prepared,
> for the sake of yourselves and other colleag-
> ues, to fight for your jobs, particularly as
> you feel you work hard for a low wage. You
> also feel that, apart from cooking the actual
> dinners, you are a great help in other ways to
> the school. A meeting has been arranged, at
> which all the interested parties will be re-
> presented, to debate the issue before a final
> decision is made by the full county council.
> The education committee will argue strongly
> that a move towards cutting back the school
> dinner service and a shorter school day is the
> only sensible strategy at a time when cuts are
> inevitable.
> What arguments do you anticipate the education
> committee will use in order to try to force
> your redundancies?
> What arguments will you use in order to change
> their minds?

The supposition is that the groups, while they
will have to thrash out the most powerful arguments
to present at the final meeting, will speak with one
voice at that meeting, thus there will be no defect-
ions. Each group may choose to select one member to
present their views or may choose to specialise in
presenting one argument each. Thus, one dinner lady
may support the cause with dietetic evidence, another may promote the supervisory service offered, and
so forth.

The Scene Enacted

The groups can present their arguments, in role, to
a final meeting involving the whole class, or, where
the teacher feels this is going to cause organisa-

tional problems and inhibit some pupils, the groups
can split to form new groups each containing a representative from the original ones so that the role
play will take place in a more intimate committee.
Where the debate involves a whole class meeting, the
teacher may decide which groups have presented their
arguments most clearly and convincingly, or the
class, having presented their cases, may stand back
to assess more objectively the quality of what they
have heard. Alternatively, the teacher may include
an 'objective observer' in each of the original
groups who will become the 'floor' in the final
meeting and will present their own questions and
objections and may be called upon to vote for or
against the proposal, and to assess the arguments
they have heard.

Many teachers will be happy to end the role
simulation exercise with an informal post mortem,
pinpointing key moments and successful tactics in
the debate. Others will wish to exploit the knowledge gained, in associated written work, though
there is obviously a danger of destroying the interest of the dynamic cut and thrust of debating
with a return to the exercise book. An acceptable
compromise lies in the classroom broadsheet, where
each group produces its own policy and propoganda
handout, to be displayed in classroom or corridor.
That produced by the school dinner ladies, for
example, might include a slogan, a description of
their plight as they see it , a line by line summary
of their claim for public support, a chronological
resume of recent events, an interview with a local
politician and a union leader who are both champ-
ioning the cause for different reasons, a 'day in
the life of a school dinner lady' article, a ver-
batim and touching tribute from a pupil, and a
report from a dietician at the local college. It
might end with a deliberately emotive warning of the
dangers of a return to the dark ages of malnutrition
and neglect. The content of the broadsheets will be
deliberately persuasive and propogandist, the kind
of engaged writing which tends to be neglected in
the English exercise book, which is generally filled
with descriptive, narrative and routinely functional
prose.

Like much in life, role simulations of the sort
described are competitive and are all the better for
that . In the past competition has sometimes been
seen as a dirty word in teaching, trailing the sins
of payment by results and the insensitive distribution of punishments and prizes. Drama helps the

teacher of English to explore the healthier side of competition, which goes hand in hand with motivation and commitment and is part of getting on and making progress in real life. Simulation exercises take pupils nearer the truth that there may not be a single right or wrong way, but there may well be a right or wrong way of presenting arguments in the context in which you find yourself. They extend the language frontiers beyond the four walls of the classroom and yet, by bedding language firmly in a recognisable and relevant context, give pupils the security they need to develop and manifest their language potential.

NOTES

1. H.M. Inspectorate, Curriculum 11-16 Working Papers (D.E.S., 1977).
2. Kate Fleming and John Miller, 'Aspects of Drama in the Middle Years Curriculum' in Michael Raggett and Malcolm Clarkson (eds.), Teaching the Eights to Thirteens, Volume 2 (Ward Lock Educational, 1976).
3. See, for example, Tony Penman and Al Wolff, Web of Language (Oxford University Press, 1981). Steve Goldenberg et al, Language (The English Programme, Thames Television in association with Hutchinson). Mike Raleigh, The Languages Book (ILEA English Centre, 1981).
4. L.S. Vygotsky, Thought and Language (MIT Press, 1962).
5. M.E. Wilt, A Study of Teacher Awareness of Listening as a Factor in Elementary Education (Journal of Educational Research, 43, 1950).
6. Andrew Wilkinson, Leslie Stratta and Peter Dudley, The Quality of Listening (Macmillan, 1974).
7. See note 3.
8. See note 3: Reproduced in Language (The English Programme).
9. See, for example, Michael Lynch, It's Your Choice : Six Role-Playing Exercises (Edward Arnold, 1977).

Chapter Four

STIMULATING WRITTEN WORK

THE DRAMA - WRITING RELATIONSHIP

Before making any practical attempts to link drama
and written work it is important to consider the
nature of the relationship between the two, for it
is easy to force and distort this, to push too much
writing into dramatic performance or kill the enjoyment of successful improvisation with a predictable
written coda. Any English written work must have
sufficient stimulus and justification, and not
every, nor even most written assignments should be
exploited in drama work and similarly, not every
piece of drama work should lead inexorably into a
piece of writing. The Schools Council Writing
across the Curriculum Project[1] confirmed that a
frighteningly narrow range of transactional writing
rules secondary school work and that far too much
routine and unstimulating writing dominates all
lessons. Thus, if we are to invite our pupils to
write we must ensure that we have good reasons for
doing so. Writing should not be seen merely as a
time-filler or control mechanism and we must provide sufficient choices of topics and styles so that
no one kind of writing, whether the story, the exercise, the summary or note-making, predominates at
the expense of other types.
     Where pupils' imaginative writing is concerned,
it is easy to see why the short story has tended to
dominate English lessons, if only because of its
convenient length and because it is almost entirely
absent elsewhere in the curriculum, and thus is a
genre which English teachers can claim as their own.
Pupils' written work must, however, encompass much
more than the short story, a form which is in any
case notoriously demanding if it is to be done well.
Pupils should meet and experiment with every kind of

prose, poetry and drama during the course of their school careers. They should, in line with the recommendations made in Chapter Three, experiment with writing which explains, criticises, analyses, compares, directs, monitors, justifies, reflects, projects, in addition to that which tells stories.

Lists of this kind, and this is not of course exhaustive, suggest the contribution drama can make to stimulating written work, for it is both a stimulus for written work which develops from drama, and provides a goal and a reason for writing. Drama helps provide 'a strong linguistic foundation, supporting the developing written structures in which children discover how words can work for them'[2]. Drama is particularly important in providing a goal for writing, that is dramatisation, where otherwise the point of the work and thus the reward would be non-existent. It also helps to break the mould of the creative writing stereotype and provides a practice run in the vivid, dynamic, and thus more memorable, use of language. Drama helps to focus the attention, channel the imagination and has a disciplining effect in making pupils pause for thought and reflection.

Writing can be seen as a stimulus for drama work, can result from or extend drama and, finally, can review and reflect upon drama. The relationship between drama and writing has, in the past, been most commonly seen in terms of writing's role in stimulating drama work. At its crudest this has meant pupils writing a play in their exercise books, before 'performing' it in front of the class, amounting to perfunctory reading and writing exercise, rather than drama proper. Certain kinds of writing demand performance; humorous dialogue sits uneasily on the page and needs the third dimension of performance to bring it to life; persuasive writing should be tried out, not on the teacher alone, but in front of a more representative audience. At times the writing, whether informal planning notes or formal script, will be conceived with drama as the goal; at times the decision to extend and exploit the writing, via drama, will be a spontaneous or pragmatic response on the part of writer and teacher. But the drama work may equally well precede the written by-product, or accompany it. Pupils may wish to jot down the results of their drama work at the end of the lesson, or may wish to keep a running record as the work evolves. The teacher may call a temporary halt for reflective writing in order to deepen concentration, or to reveal further facets

73

of characterisation, aware that this should disclose new ideas and departures for future drama work. The teacher and pupils may wish to tie down a successful piece of improvisation by scripting the proceedings. It is difficult to draw a clear line between this writing, which extends drama, and that which reviews and reflects upon it, except that these last types may more obviously take the pupil away from his own work to review and reflect on the work of others, whether in school, in the media or in the theatre.

WRITING AS A STIMULUS FOR DRAMA

Planning notes, role play cards, scripts, poems, stories, letters, diary entries, riddles, lists, can all stimulate drama work but only a selection should and can be chosen for this purpose. The choice may be the teacher's or the pupil's, it may be spontaneous or preprogrammed, particularly where it will call upon a greater space than the ordinary classroom can provide. The writing may be exploited through drama because it seems to demand it, for example the monologue, dialogue, play script, because only by doing so will its true potential be revealed, vivid conversation within a story, the narrative poem, or in order to find a solution, perhaps where the writer is having problems deciding how the obstacles in his plot will be resolved. It is important that pupils are given a clear brief for writing, which has drama as its goal, since only then will they be helped to meet the demands of dramatisation. The following example suggests how this might be done.

A group of able second year pupils has been studying Victorian gallows literature, and particularly the final verse confessions of convicted criminals. The teacher is loath to do the obvious and suggest that pupils try their hands at these, at least immediately, since the imaginative gulf between their own situation and that of these nineteenth century criminals seems too great. Instead she asks pupils to consider situations where they have, or may be called upon to review their past experiences. They suggest moments when death appears imminent and talk of their own experiences when caught on a cliff ledge or stranded out at sea or in the midst of a nightmare. They conjecture what a child might think about in the darkness of a first night at boarding school, or a prisoner in solitary confinement for the first time, or a novice

during the first night in an enclosed order. The
teacher asks them to read excerpts from a number of
recommended autobiographies which describe such
experiences and suggests that pupils write a one
act play, destined for performance or recording if
they wish, which shows a central character who is
forced to review his or her life and who hears and
converses with the voices of those nearest or dear-
est who, though absent, appear tangible and real.
The group is asked to pay particular attention to
the nature of these relationships and the way voice
texture, as well as what is said, will add to the
audience's understanding of these.

Writing which sees dramatisation as the goal
does not have to be extended : Take the case of a
group of first year pupils who have been looking at
machines, and particularly the W. Heath Robinson
variety, and at onomatopoeic descriptions for
their functions. The teacher might see this as an
opportunity for describing objectively and accurat-
ely the work of an existing or imaginary machine, as
if to someone who has never seen it before, and
might then ask pupils to devise imaginative descriptions for the sounds the different parts of the
machine make. This could logically lead into a
tableau where pupils take on the parts of the components and start to work in a predetermined way,
with appropriate noises, when the right button is
pushed.

Take the case of a class investigating the
nature of perception. 'An Ordinary Day'[3] by Norman
MacCaig begins:

> I took my mind a walk
> Or my mind took me a walk –
> Whichever was the truth of it...

and ends by observing how extraordinary is 'the
nature of the mind / And the process of observing'.
Any attempt to convey the complex process of observation and perception could well start by looking
at the role of certain familiar authority figures in
the lives of pupils: parents, teachers and the
police, for example. Pupils might write a fairly
simple dialogue, showing perhaps a parent confronting a child with a misdemeanour, in the first two
columns. The second column might be reserved for
the thoughts and feelings of those speaking, which
may elaborate or detract from what has been said,
but will certainly help to reveal the truth which
is often hidden by the spoken words. The results,

whether serious or humorous, should help to explore
the tightness of the roles in which we sometimes
constrict ourselves and the way words are sometimes
used as a blunt instrument to obscure meaning.
This should logically develop into an acting out of
the scene, as four rather than two players take the
parts, showing how each dialogue, both the real and
the suppressed, might end.

Plot-making and Play-making

Drama offers novel opportunities for exploring the
characteristics of narrative writing and for constructing narrative frameworks. Many pupils find
plot construction very difficult and tend to lean
heavily on the few plot types they trust, hence the
popularity of the 'It was only a dream after all'
device. This difficulty is in part a result of the
apparently daunting number of possibilities that
face all writers, and in part the result of famil-
iarity with only a narrow range of plot models.
When a pupil objects 'But I don't know what to write
about' he is hinting at the complexity of the task.
He may have the theme, probably suggested by the
teacher, to work on, but theme is not synonymous
with plot and he is probably unsure about how to
identify the plot options, select from them and
thence order and motivate the sequence of actions.
He may also be unaware that inspiration does not
usually appear fortuitously and magically but, like
happiness and other abstract states, needs to be
nurtured, helped along and worked at. One initial
way to break down pupils' inhibitions is to get
them telling stories in groups, in turn, a sentence
at a time or a word at a time. These oral narra-
tives are normally more disciplined alternatives to
'Consequences' or 'Chinese Whispers' which follow
the same pattern but can degenerate into apparently
frivolous time-fillers. The teacher and class can
extract from such experiments a number of feasible,
if not always naturalistic, plots, since the bizarre and the surrealistic are permissible. Such
group stories can introduce notions of the 'sub-
plot', 'motivation', the 'flash back' and other
devices.
Pupils are often surprised how many plots are
there for the pinching, and how essentially simple
many of these plots are. Little Red Riding Hood,
for example, is about a little girl who helps a
relation and is trapped by that relation's frailty
and by her own vulnerability and naivety into a
near fatal confrontation with a villain. Only the

intervention of a third party finally saves her. It is the stuff of which thrillers are made. The Three Little Pigs demonstrates how the brute strength of an enemy can be defeated by hard work and cunning. Time and again the interloper tests and overcomes the defences of the persecuted pigs before being defeated himself. It is the stuff of which Westerns are made. By borrowing and extending these and other familiar frameworks, pupils may come to realise that there is nothing underhand about borrowing, since it is the flesh and not the skeleton which lends substance. This is something that Shakespeare and other great writers have always understood, and have proved by manipulating a simple plot to produce many different plays, stories, novels and poems. One way into such an exploration might be to feed generalised plot descriptions, such as the two above, to pupils, with the clue that they come from popular children's stories, before asking them to translate other well known stories into similar plot descriptions. Pupils could then transform a story such as The Ugly Duckling into a contemporary play, substituting realistic human beings and situations for those in the original. This story or that of The Seven Dwarfs make good selections, since they allow scope for satire, but the result may be serious or humorous. Pupils may wish to keep the 'Listen with Mother' tone by including a narrator or commentator, to press home the point that, while the setting may be realistic, this is part allegory, part fable.

Pupils may be helped to see possible plot options by discussing (and then working out through drama) how a deliberately truncated story line could be realistically completed, and then justifying their conclusions. This is similar to, though less mechanical than sequencing procedures. Pupils can move on to construct their own whodunnit plots, identifying and borrowing some of the classic devices of established crime writers. All pupils should eventually be able to identify broad types of plots : the quest or journey type epitomised by Arthurian tales, Bunyan's 'The Pilgrim's Progress' and picaresque novels; the bargain plot, where a price must eventually be paid, seen in the Doctor Faust legend and many fairy stories; the whodunnit; the disaster plot where characters try to extricate themselves from an initial catastrophe, for example, Kafka's 'The Trial', Arthur Haley's 'Airport', John Wyndham's 'The Day of the Triffids; the conventional romance, described at its simplest as 'girl meets boy, girl loses boy, girl gets boy'; the unfolding of true, or supposedly true chronological events, seen in the biography or autobiography. These represent a selection from the major discernible plot types, but of course they are not mutually exclusive, thus a writer of Dickens' stature can successfully combine a major plot and several sub-plots which incorporate romance, a journey and a detective story, ('Bleak House' is a good example). Pupils can experiment with perhaps the simplest, certainly the earliest novel plot type, that which takes the leading character or characters on a journey, a type favoured by Defoe, Fielding, Smollett and still popular with contemporary novelists and writers of chidren's fiction. Pupils might use Ibsen's 'Peer Gynt', 'The Pilgrim's Progress' or the medieval morality play 'Everyman', as inspiration for writing and thence drama, which seeks to show the moral dilemmas that a modern teenager faces.

For those who find even the journey type of plot a difficult one to sustain, the Mummers' Play with its comforting stability and simplicity may provide a suitable alternative model for writing and drama. Here a simplified and ritualised confrontation, that involving the Turkish Knight and Saint George, is displayed. Right and might triumph magnanimously and a rich variety of accompanying characters quarrel and make up on the side lines and comment upon themselves, each other and the combatants. Pupils might adopt this model to show how different agencies and individuals might comment on, or involve themselves in a confrontation on the football terrace, in the home, or on the streets. Such writing lends itself to ritualised performance, where movement is less important than the verve with which the words are delivered, and where, as the mummers discovered, much can be done in a limited space. It is important to stress that it is not imitation we are after but imaginative manipulation of a basic model, so that while the final products will share a common framework, they will all be different in substance.

It is dangerously tempting to assume that because a story or poem has a strong narrative line that it must be dramatised. Unless the dramatisation adds to an understanding of the story, the characters and the issues involved, it is not justified. However, there are occasions when pupils' written work, just like their questions, will raise issues which are not fully explored, perhaps because of a lack of expertise, understanding or length. In the following example a first year pupil has written a very abrupt story about a stranger who moves into a haunted house in a village. The house has remained empty and its strange sounds have scared neighbours for some time. Soon after the stranger has moved in, the ghost of an old man haunts him and then suddenly disappears. The man marks the spot at which the ghost vanished and next day asks a servant to dig at the spot. They find the body of a young woman and ask the village vicar and priest to identify the corpse. Startled, they confirm that she is the squire's daughter who disappeared in mysterious circumstances many years before. An old tramp who wandered the village was presumed to have murdered her and, though there was no proof, he was hounded out of the village and was later found dying of hunger in a ditch. Forensic evidence suggests that only the original owner of the house could have murdered the young lady. The tramp is reburied in consecrated ground and never haunts the house again.

The teacher recognises the story's debt to a tale told by Pliny, a translation of which appears in one of the class text books[4]. The teacher is pleased to see that the pupil has elaborated the original ending but notices that many creative opportunities have been missed. He goes to write 'Too short' at the end but realises that this is hardly correct, since what is missing is the sort of detailed annotation which will bring scenes and characters to life. He feels that the only way to demonstrate these possibilities is to take the story apart and reassemble it with the aid of drama. The teacher reads the story to the class and praises its potential. He first asks the class to identify all the characters involved. They suggest: the house owner, the servant, the ghost, the vicar and the doctor. The teacher then asks, 'But what other characters are suggested in the story?'. The pupils suggest the neighbours, an estate agent, a grave digger. Finally, the teacher asks whether there are any other characters the class might wish to list, to add interest to the story. They suggest the house owner's friend, a journalist from the local newspaper, and the tramp, the squire and his daughter seen in a flash back scene. The teacher gives each pair of pupils a copy of the plot, divided by short vertical lines into sections. The first section reads: 'A stranger comes to a village and buys a house in which to live. The house is haunted and has remained empty for many years. The villagers are frightened by its reputation and by

the strange noises that come from it after dark'.
Pupils are asked to identify, discuss, and then
list all the questions which this brief introduction
leaves unanswered. In other words they are asked to
stretch its imaginative possibilities to the limit.
The teacher gives an example of an obvious question,
'Who is the stranger?'. The class suggest the factors involved in answering it; they will need to
decide the stranger's sex, name, age, appearance,
personality, occupation, interests, family and reasons for moving to the village. The teacher alerts
the class to the possibilities they may miss, for
example, the word 'buys' : from whom? Does the
agent, estate agent, vendor deceive him or does he
admit that the house is haunted? Is the stranger
happy to buy a haunted house? What sales techniques does the seller use? Once they have settled
on interesting and convincing answers to these
questions, the pupils jot down their new 'stretched'
version of the original, which is now less plot
than imaginative story. They use this as a basis,
not for a script, which the teacher fears may
unnecessarily constrict the drama work which is to
follow, but for a scenario which has dramatisation
as its goal. Thus one pair of pupils produces the
following for Scene One:

> We see the stranger, Mr. Henry Mathews, reading
> a large book in a library. He tells the lib-
> rarian he is investigating some unsolved local
> mysteries. He has come across one which happ-
> ened in a village called Little Aston a hun-
> dred years ago. He asks the librarian if she
> knows any more about it. She says he could
> visit the village and the vicar to find out
> more.

This exercise helps pupils to confront a problem
that all playwrights face, that of giving necessary
information to an audience without making the exposition tedious and unrealistic. Since there will
not be time, nor the personnel for every pair to
act out the whole of their interpretation, and since
the point of the exercise is to suggest the many
possibilities which are latent in any bare plot,
rather than polished performance, the teacher asks
pupils to form groups of four. These groups select
any one scene from their scenarii which interests
them and is dramatically feasible. They use this
as a basis for dramatic improvisation, sometimes
refining the orginal scenario in the light of their

work. The teacher asks certain groups to share
part of their work with the rest of the class and
then asks them to describe, without reading their
scenarii, how this fits into their interpretation
of the story.

The Commedia dell'Arte

The approaches outlined above work by taking a plot
and superimposing the characters upon it. However,
it is perfectly possible to reverse the process,
working from a predetermined group of characters
to a plot. This is of course how the Commedia
dell'Arte of the sixteenth and seventeenth centur-
ies operated. The Commedia, like some small repertory companies today, was based upon a group of
actors who specialised in stock roles with their
own stock speeches, which could be adapted to fit
the occasion. The cast list included, Arlecchino
(Harlequin) a cunning and nimble rascal; Pantalone,
a mean and somewhat ridiculous old man, whether
father, husband or bachelor; the Captain, a boaster
and coward (the Miles Gloriosus); the Doctor, an
interfering and pompous lawyer or physician;
Pedrolino, the young male lover, who is rather fee-
ble and love sick; his loved one, known by a variety
of names, beautiful and sought after; her maid,
often called Columbina (Columbine), shrewd and witty,
she helps the young lovers and plot along. The
Commedia's great value for the teacher of English
and drama is that it provides a very useful model
for drama work and, from the literary point of view,
offers an excellent introduction to commedy's many
aspects, that of Aristophanes, Plautus, Terence
and Shakespeare, and more generally, the comedy of
humours, of manners, slapstick, satire, farce, and
black comedy. It provides a model which can be
feasibly exploited in drama lessons, that of a
small number of actors who relied not on a script
but on scenarii which formed a basis for improvised
dialogue. The staging was simple and the identity
of the characters could be reinforced, if need be,
by very simple details of costume or the nature of
their masks. The Commedia introduces the idea of
informal 'repertory' groups where pupils can agree
to specialise in certain roles and where the teacher
can devolve authority and decision-making to the
group. It helps to develop particular areas of
expertise while allowing individuals the opportunity
to experiment with a variety of interpretations and
skills and encourages pupils to think about the
whole range of possibilities which might be opened

up by simply linking a range of predetermined characters. It is a model which works well with any
age group, provided the work is sufficiently structured and the guidelines are made sufficiently
clear:

   There is no need, particularly where younger
pupils are concerned, to mention the Commedia dell'
Arte as such, until its way of working is understood. The teacher might instead 'introduce' the
stock characters, with the help of masks. These
characters can be loosely based on the Commedia
types and might include: a cantankerous and ridiculous old man; a servant who is clever and cunning
but likeable; a rascal; a boaster; a young man who
is in love; and the one he loves. As in the Commedia, players will be able to take on more than
one role if appropriate, and the male-female mix
can be adjusted to meet the needs of the repertory
group. The class, in groups of five or six, can
then discuss what they are to make, by way of plot,
from this raw material, and can develop role descriptions or role cards, filling out the characters
they have been given or have chosen. At first they
may find it easiest simply to see these characters
as types, even as caricatures, and need not feel
uneasy if the plot is rather mechanical. Pupils
should begin by concentrating on the early scenes,
focussing on the identification of the personalities and problems of those involved. It may
help if the teacher gives them an initial push into
the first scene: 'Let's suppose that the old man
wishes to marry his daughter to a rich but foolish
boaster, when she is secretly in love with the
young son of their neighbour...'; 'Let's imagine
that a rascal wishes to deceive a foolish old man
into paying a small fortune for the secret of a
worthless invention...'. Other pupils may need a
firmer basis for the improvisation and the teacher
may circulate a story line which the groups then
dismember, describing and annotating each scene
at greater length. The male-female mix can be
adapted to suit the needs of each group:
Character (A) is convinced that young lady (B) is
infatuated with him but that she is too shy to
suggest her love. He discusses his problem with a
friend (C), who suggests writing her a letter. (A)
does, but it is entrusted to a simpleton (D) who,
confused by the numbers on the street doors, delivers the letter to the wrong house. (The letter
begins, 'My dear love...'). The letter is read by
a middle-aged woman (E) and shocked, but also

secretly flattered by these advances, she persuades
her elderly husband (F) to confront (A). Friend
(C) reveals to the audience his love for (B) and
his determination to destroy (A)'s chances with her.
To this end he bolsters (F)'s courage for a fight
with (A). The two prepare to fight but are interrupted without injury when (A) sees (B) pass by in
conversation with (C). (A) is snubbed by (B) who
denies all knowledge of the letter. (F) accuses
(A) of being a philanderer and (A) has to be rude
about (E) in order to convince (F) that he does not
love her. (E) overhears and knocks (A) out. (G),
who is (B)'s maid, takes pity on (A), revives him
and leads him to her kitchen where, bandaged and
helpless, her mistress does not recognise him and
comes to like him. (F) sees his wife talking to
(C), since she now wishes to make it up with (A).
(F) draws the wrong conclusions and advertises his
wife's supposed infidelity with (C). (B), aware
now of (C)'s duplicity, agrees to marry (A).
This is merely a model for what can be done with
a small number of players. It is useful in that it
simplifies improvisation, since only two players
need be 'on stage' for much of the action. The
plot may be handed to pupils complete, alternatively
the more that is cut from the end, the greater the
challenge to pupils to devise their own denouement.

Only after pupils have found their feet in
exploiting their own and the teacher's plots, will
they be in a position to recognise these characters
as the types they will undoubtedly be in early
improvisations. Only then can they return to the
characters to delve below the surface, to identify
the questions which remain unanswered and which
lend greater complexity to each one : Why should
the old man be mean with his money? Does he behave
in a similar way to everyone he meets? How do the
other characters perceive him? Pupils might stretch
the possibilities suggested by the characters they
have been given or chosen, placing them not together
in place or time but deciding that they co-exist in
time but live in different environments, or may
have all shared an environment, perhaps a house,
but have all lived in it at different times. Alternatively, the group may translate their types into
contemporary terms : the city stockbroker, a football supporter, a char lady, a punk rocker, a
member of the royal family, an old person. The
teacher might ask the class to describe the stereotypes attached to these and then show them in action
as they wait nervously in a state of limbo after

death, in an imaginary waiting room. A strange
noise prompts them to break their silence and reveal their stereotyped selves to each other. Pupils
may then choose to focus on one character at a time,
showing him or her in other circumstances, and breaking through the stereotype to show unexpected
facets of personality.

WRITING AS THE PRODUCT OR EXTENSION OF DRAMA WORK

Writing may be used to deepen the drama experience,
to broaden it, discipline it, or all three. It may
describe what has been achieved or not achieved,
distil the work of a lesson, describe what is
happening, attempt to get under the skin of a
character, present an alternative interpretation,
move the action back or forth in time, provide
written accompaniment for a piece of mime, or describe how it felt to be playing a part. Writing
may be by-product or ultimate goal, to be treasured
or displayed, or rough draft and disposable.

Poetry
Drama may be particularly useful in stimulating the
expression of feelings, and thus of poetry. Many
teachers are, perhaps understandably, wary of asking pupils to write poetry because of the difficulties associated with its form and because of its
reputation for being obscure, irrelevant or 'sissy'.
Too often we ask pupils to write poetry when it
appears to them that they lack the significant experiences to fuel it. Drama focuses attention on
what words can do, mean, say, and at its best it
should encourage pupils to risk using words which
humdrum experiences may not allow scope for. It
allows pupils to take on the identity of another
and to hide behind the words of another, if need be.
     The 'frozen action' technique may be used to
freeze a piece of improvisation as a tableau; pupils
may describe and record what they see in words and
images. By sharing their jottings, pupils may come
to realise the range of perception which is possible.
It may also suggest that the raw material for poetry is all around them. A tape recorder, particularly where its presence is undisclosed, which records
a successful piece of dialogue may surprise pupils
by revealing the inventiveness of much of their work
and should give them the confidence to try new
departures in their written work.
     Teachers of English spend a great deal of time,
sometimes vainly, attempting to broaden the descrip-

tive vocabulary of their pupils. One need only
consider the exercises which invite pupils to think
of synonyms for 'nice' or the comments in red ink
in the margin, 'Find a better word'. When we introduce 'better words' in the classroom too often they
are lost since they are merely introduced and not
indelibly linked with a vivid memory. Drama can
be invaluable in exploring, through movement and
gesture, the meaning and impact of these words.
One way of encouraging particularly younger pupils
to see the finer nuances of meaning which distinguish words, is to give different groups of pupils
different groups of words which they must illustrate through mime. Pupils might be given the verb
'go'; they then list the words which are similar
to the key verb but are less generalised and more
descriptive, for example, saunter, stagger, wander,
slither, march...They may illustrate each word for
other groups who are asked to identify it. The
audience may then be asked to nominate common and
proper nouns and images to fit each verb and ill-
ustration. Pupils can then write up the results
as a series of descriptive lines, which may or may
not form the basis for a poem:

> I stagger from my bed in the dark,
> The water trickles through my hands,
> The ketchup oozes on my plate,
> Dead leaves scatter from the path,
> A pigeon flutters through the trees,
> My brother lurches to the gate,
> I dawdle 'till I'm late.   (Pupil)

Pupils can then experiment with these verbs, moving
them around in their writing to gauge the effect:

> I ooze from my bed in the dark,
> The water dawdles through my hands,
> The ketchup scatters on my plate,
> Dead leaves flutter from the path,
> A pigeon lurches through the trees,
> My brother trickles to the gate,
> I stagger 'till I'm late.

Characterisation

Drama, as we have seen, can help to uncover facets
of character which might otherwise remain undisclosed. Writing which follows such an exploration can
consolidate what has been revealed and form the
basis for future more demanding drama work and the
portrayal of more complex characters in writing.

One way into revealing new characters is to put pupils into positions where they are forced to conjure up identities from their own imagination or experiences. This might start by asking pupils to think of situations where members of the public are interviewed for the purpose of filling in a form. It should soon become clear to pupils that it is almost impossible to take any meaningful step in life without filling in a form. Pupils, in pairs, can then consider and discuss the sorts of questions which their chosen form would need to ask. The questions may be written down by the interviewer at this stage though sometimes spontaneous improvisation rather th a reading out yields more lively results. The inter viewee may fix his identity before the questions are asked or may trust to chance and imagination. Again the latter option sometimes throws up more intriguin and orginal details than pre-programmed answers. Pupils may then swop roles or choose one or more other kinds of forms. They can profitably share their work with others so that a whole range of new identities is revealed. This exercise is unlikely on its own to reveal all the facets of personality, but if the improvisation is working well and if the participants and audience are prepared to build on the hints that are there, a more three dimensional character should emerge. To this end, the audience may be encouraged to ask questions of those interviewed to find out more. Where these answers appear to be at odds with other earlier information, the audience can bring attention to it and ask the inter viewee to explain the apparent discrepancy. The teacher may invite pairs of pupils to put the same character in another quite distinct and perhaps less formal interview situation where new information wil come to light, for example, in a marriage guidance clinic, in the doctor's consulting room or at home, where the character must face the family's questions

We owe it to our pupils to give them sufficient options for writing, and to allow them to map out writing assignments well in advance. One positive way of using the occasional drama period is to use it as a testing ground, a time for experimentation, which should stimulate a wide range of writing. In the following example, a fourth year C.S.E. group is encouraged by the teacher to nominate the homework assignments for the fortnight ahead, which will eventually go to make up their English folders. A group of four girls who are not sure what to suggest but know that they wish to work on it in drama too, approach the teacher with a request for a theme. He suggests they begin with a simple idea, a family, and then produce role cards for each member of the family. They can then throw these characters together in an improvisation in the next drama lesson, when other groups of pupils will be using part of the time to work out their own ideas, which have also been agreed in advance with the teacher. He suggests a simple scene to get the girls started : the family sheltering from the rain in a seaside cafe. The group adds its own ideas : sitting in a cinema, opening presents on Christmas morning, visiting a member of the family in hospital, and buying a car. The characters soon emerge from these scenes as distinct individuals with their own voices, opinions and habits. The first written product of the drama lesson is a list of associated ideas for writing, which immediately occur to the group : a description of the process of improvisation; a polished script based on the improvisation; letters or diary entries written as if by the characters, showing their different perceptions of what they have experienced; letters of complaint, thanks, invitation, to friends, business agencies, to the press; replies to letters received; a poem, essay, story or lyrics written by a member of the family as a competition entry; a statement made to a police officer; a job application with curriculum vitae and references; a newspaper article featuring one of the family, for example, a review of an amateur drama production, a description of a wedding or court case. The group soon has a long list and the teacher suggests they each select three to five assignments from it which represent different kinds of writing. He suggests they begin by producing an imaginary census form which will summarise the basic data and will form a basis for the work which is to follow. Once the girls begin to write their first rough drafts they discover, with pleasure, that the writing they are undertaking is distinct from the routine; here they can choose the 'voice' for their words, thus the content, tone and style of a letter or poem written by Granny will obviously differ from that produced by the youngest member of the family. The finished assignments represent not only a range of types of writing but also a range of voices and perspectives and, for once, the experiences that are probed go beyond the writers' horizons.

In this second example, the teacher of an able second year class is, without fuss and preamble, introducing them to Shakespeare with the intention of exploring his relevance for a twentieth century

reader. To this end, she selects those extracts
which can be lifted from the text with the minimum
of injury and distortion to the meaning. The selection includes Jaques' famous speech from Act II
Scene VII of 'As You Like It':

> All the worlds's a stage,
> And all the men and women merely players;
> They have their exits and their entrances;
> And one man in his time plays many parts,
> His acts being seven ages. At first the infant,
> Mewling and puking in the nurse's arms;
> Then the whining school-boy, with his satchel
> And shining morning face, creeping like a snail
> Unwillingly to school. And then the lover,
> Sighing like a furnace, with a woeful ballad
> Made to his mistress' eyebrow...

The teacher first reads the complete speech with
expression and with expansive and amusing gestures
in order to convey as much of the meaning as possible, since she has warned the class that she will
be asking them to treat the speech very much like
a crossword puzzle; that is, working in small groups,
they will note the meaning of all the words and phrases they think they can understand and will under-
line, on their duplicated copies, those they cannot.
This group 'comprehension' exercise is followed by a
plenary session where group spokesmen offer meanings
to the rest of the class. The teacher asks each
pupil to complete and write up their own paraphrase,
since it will be needed for what is to follow. In
the next drama lesson the class is divided into
'acting companies' of five or six. The teacher
explains that Shakespeare would have been used to
working with a small, tightly knit group of actors.
Each company is asked to illustrate a reading of the
original speech with the aid of actors who will play
the parts of nurse, school boy, lovers, soldier,
justice and old men. The class is then asked to
imagine that they are a latter day Jaques, commenting on contemporary mankind. They are asked to
decide in what ways Jaques' view is inevitably a
limited one and how a twentieth century perspective
might differ from that presented in the original.
The pupils conclude that, despite the language which
fixes the speech in Shakespeare's time, the portraits
are surprisingly topical and universal. One group of
girls does though identify that this is a speech
delivered by a man and describing men, despite the
introductory reference to 'men and women'. The

teacher invites the class, working in pairs, or
alone, to rewrite the original giving it a more up
to date feel. They will have the opportunity to
present their versions, either as a speech or piece
of poetry to be read aloud and displayed, or as a
mime with an accompanying narrator, or as a performance with dialogue, with the narrator as an option-
al extra.

In the final example, a group of third year
pupils have been investigating early man's attempts
to explain natural phenomena through stories, thus
they have looked at different flood myths, at Greek
creation myths and at legendary characters such as
King Arthur and Robin Hood and have tried to suggest
why and how kernals of truth should be elaborated in
this way. The group has tried to analyse why apo-
cryphal stories should take root even today, with
the help of an ITV 'Middle English' broadcast. The
teacher then asks, 'Are we too sophisticated to need
legends today?'. The group relates its answer to
two films which many in the class have seen : Ken
Russell's 'Tommy' which describes, in deliberately
exaggerated terms, the rise to fame of a deaf, dumb
and blind boy who becomes a cult figure for his
adoring young fans, and the Monty Python team's
'Life of Brian' which substitutes an only too fallible Brian for Christ and, in the process, demonstrates how legends can be manufactured for those
who are desperate to believe. The group concludes
that if modern legendary characters are to emerge
they are more likely to do so within the fields of
entertainment and sport. They also suggest that
legends tend to emerge in retrospect and that much
is forgiven, particularly when the famous die young.
The teacher asks the pupils to imagine that a retro-
spective documentary tribute is being made at the
end of the twentieth century to a sportsman or
entertainer who may be entirely the product of the
pupil's imagination or may be based loosely on a
real person. The programme will contain a television
interview, featuring the celebrity at the height of
his or her fame, intended as a publicity exercise
which will eulogize rather than expose and thus
will carefully ignore anything which detracts from
the myth. Working in pairs, the interviewer and
celebrity map out certain key areas for questioning,
aware that any faux pas can be 'edited' later. Both
pupils emerge from this with a greater understanding
of what they now know, and as significantly, do not
know about their chosen character. At the beginning of the next lesson the teacher tells the group

that they are going to explore how 'legends' and
thus people can be packaged and sold as commercially
as any inanimate product. He introduces, and the
class discusses, the term 'hype' and they relate it
to the selling of records, films and books, in particular. Pupils collect and bring in articles describing the rise to fame of current celebrities;
these are displayed in the classroom. Pupils are
told that they are going to explore how an ordinary
individual, with no more than average talents, can
be transformed into what his or her publicist or
agent will describe as a 'living legend'. The group
can draw upon their earlier drama work and, to make
the job of fleshing out the story that much easier,
the teacher gives each pupil a sheet of paper with
the following sub-headings, on to which they can
jot their initial ideas:

'A Living Legend'

Real name:

Place of birth: Date of
                                   Birth:

Family background:

Childhood and adolescence:
appearance, personality and experiences:

Early manifestations of talents (if any):

Initial breakthrough:

Rise to fame:

Relationships with family, friends, fans
and colleagues:

Greatest accolades and
achievements:

<u>Most quoted/misquoted remarks</u>:

<u>The fall from fortune</u>:

The teacher asks pupils to suggest the kinds of
details that might be included under these categories but stresses that the headings are intended as
no more than sign-posts and can be changed if they
are found to be constricting. Without mentioning
Chaucer's name, the teacher introduces the Chaucer-
ian concept of tragedy and the wheel of fortune.
He tells the group that, if it suits their purposes,
they can imagine the life of the celebrity as being
like a wheel which carries him to the pinnacle of
fame but cannot maintain him there for ever. Each
original pair of pupils pools their ideas to produce
a completed sheet, before joining up with another
pair. From this discussion one 'legend' emerges
which the group will develop through drama. They
are asked to choose and develop one scene prior to
the point of greatest success, and one scene which
captures a moment after this point and showing, in
both cases, the celebrity's relationships with those
around him. Some pupils choose to contrast their
earlier, distorted interview with a later, more
candid programme which features interviews with
those who knew him, after his death. Some show
the celebrity as he watches a television report of
his exploits; others show how he emerged on the entertainment scene with just the right image at just
the right time, only to be ignored when the next
cult figure is pushed into the limelight. Some see
him as innocent and manipulated, others as vain and
opportunist. In the process of their work, all
pupils take a closer look at how modern myths may
develop and at the role of the media in marketing
and image-making.

WRITING WHICH REVIEWS OR REFLECTS UPON DRAMA WORK

This type of writing may interpret what has been
seen or done, assess it and reflect upon it.
Chapter Seven will consider in more detail how
pupils may reflect upon and assess the drama work of
others, here I intend merely to outline the kinds
of writing which might, occasionally, review and
reflect upon curricular drama. This writing will
not emerge in a vacuum but will be the result of
reflective and reviewing talk both during and after

the drama work. It should, like all writing, serve a purpose, perhaps to focus critical faculties in a way which is not always possible in the hurly burly of a drama lesson, act as a first step towards criticising the work of professionals, or produce a permanent record of something which is ephemeral.

Pupils may describe why they choose to interpret a part in a particular way, how they felt when they were confronted with a view point at variance with their own; they may record the imaginative leap and conjecture, using their drama work as a basis, how it feels to be disabled, deformed, discriminated against, lonely, ignored, old and infirm. The more choice we give to our pupils the more they will have to talk and write about, since the greater will be the need to justify and describe their decisions, rather than merely accepting the teacher's instructions as immutable. Those pupils who are faced with a problem, perhaps deciding a convincing denouement for a narrative thread, may find writing about why and how they resolved the problem as they did a challenging experience, an aid in writing future stories or plays and in assessing the fiction of others. Recording mistakes in interpretation and presentation, ('We made a mess of it because...'), may help pupils to see the drama process in terms of the medium, what works and what does not, and may help them in the future to write successfully with drama in mind.

NOTES

1. See: Nancy Martin et al, Writing and Learning Across the Curriculum (Ward Lock Educational, 1976).
2. Tom Stabler, Drama in Primary Schools, Schools Council Drama 5 - 11 Project (Macmillan, 1978
3. Geoffrey Summerfield (ed.), reprinted in Junior Voices, the fourth book, (Penguin Education 1970).
4. See: Barry Maybury, Wordspinners (Oxford University Press, 1981).

Chapter Five

TO AND FROM THE SET TEXT

The set text can be defined as the class or group
reader which is set by the teacher for study, or as
the text set for examination at C.S.E., 16+, 'O' or
'A' Level, by an external examining board. In
either case the aim must be to encourage pupils'
understanding of these texts through their reading
of them, which should be both pleasurable and
active. That is, they provide the material on which
pupils will try their critical skills, asking questions of the text, of the characters, and bringing
to the pages their own experiences and understanding
of human relationships. Far from wilting, intimidated by the prospect of 'literature', pupils will
need to articulate their own grasp of how the raw
material of action and speech have been significantly shaped by the writer.
    The class reader or examination text offers an
organisational focal point for a programme of English work, providing order and coherency where
otherwise vacillation and fragmentation might be a
danger. All other English work can be gathered
under the mantle of the text:

      After a half term's work on "Smith" our class-
      room was awash with stories about being "on the
      run", snow poems, highwayman songs, monographs
      on Wren and Dick Turpin, imaginary accounts of
      life in Newgate, the history of Toby Jugs,
      research into street cries, a group-written
      newspaper set in period, and designs for
      special household aids for the blind. Drama
      lessons included trust games, and a dramatiz-
      ation of a courtroom scene. Underpinning all
      this was plenty of language work of all kinds,
      drawn from Garfield's extraordinarily vivid
      style.[1]

To and From the Set Text

In the hands of an enlightened and well-organised
teacher, as here, the class reader works well, but
the dangers of overkill are obvious, particularly
where a routine approach is taken to the reading of
the text, and the class know that they have little
to look forward to but many weeks of tedious reading
around the class, frustratingly punctuated by
literal comprehension questions.

As the quotation suggests, drama has much to
offer in the modest sense of injecting some variety
into an approach to the class reader. Thus, understanding becomes not simply a matter of oral or
written comprehension questions but is broadened to
include a three dimensional realisation of the
issues involved. In addition, drama provides a
means for exploring the differences between prose
and play and for discovering the principles involved
in transforming the first into the second:

> ...drama is a transforming agent, allowing
> children to identify with story characters and
> achieve a more active experience through the
> freedom to initiate and not simply imitate...
> Story may take on added life and meaning when
> it becomes more than something read or listened
> to but yields its content, characters and
> issues for children to work upon and extend.[2]

These are broad descriptions of drama's role in
clarifying and probing the set text; each teacher
will use it in a different way, depending on his
objectives for a particular lesson, or pupil, as the
examples which follow seek to demonstrate.

TO AND FROM THE CLASS READER

The 'To and From' of the title demands some explanation: Drama work which seeks to focus attention on
particular themes which are of importance in the
book, explore options for action which must have
faced the writer when constructing the plot, anticipate the moral issues involved, or relate pupils'
experiences to those they will read about, can be
said to move 'to' the class reader. While drama
work which sees certain confrontations or conversa-
tions in the text as being particularly 'dramatic',
in seeming to call for dramatic realisation, or work
which attempts to throw light on the obscure and
unfamiliar in the text, can be seen to move 'from'
the class reader.

There is no class reader which is totally unfit

for dramatisation (as a recent BBC interpretation of
'To the Lighthouse' has reaffirmed) but some are
more immediately suited than others, and particularly those with a strong narrative thread which raise
universal, topical or contentious issues. Collec-
tions of myths have become favoured class readers in
the top junior and bottom secondary years for a number of reasons. They are part of our cultural
heritage and thus are academically 'respectable';
they describe those phenomena which tend to appeal
to pupils in this age range, the supernatural and
the gruesome, vivid protagonists, and simplified
struggles between good and evil; and they come in
conveniently short sections. This hardly does
justice to the subtlety and complexity of some of
the tales, but these are ingredients which undoubtedly attract English and drama teachers and their
pupils to the Greek, Egyptian, Norse and Arthurian
myths.

'Tales of the Greek Heroes'
It would be easy to read Roger Lancelyn Green's
retelling of the 'Tales of the Greek Heroes'[3] one
chapter and one lesson at a time, bogging down the
issues and incidents in questions and answers concerning the characteristics of each of the unfamiliar deities. Such an approach might help pupils
to translate the Greek gods' names into their Latin
equivalents but it would probably eclipse the impact
of the characters and fail to explore the need for
such myths. The two examples which follow describe
how two teachers of two different first year secondary classes approach these tales. They share the
same aim, to increase understanding with the aid of
drama, but have their own objectives to guide the
course of their lessons.
     In the first example the teacher wishes to use
drama to direct the pupils' reading of the text. He
is aware that an unthinking approach to the descriptive introduction to the tales may immediately
alienate those, and particularly the less able, who
find the foreign names and location intimidating and
obscure. He decides to focus the work around the
Prometheus myth and aims, in the first lesson, to
introduce the major protagonists in as vivid a way
as possible. The class has become accustomed to the
teacher's sporadic appearances in role. On this
occasion he enters in an elaborate mask and introduces himself as Zeus, King of the Gods and of
Olympus. He describes Olympus and then calls on his
'brothers and sisters' to take their rightful places

alongside him, first Hera, Queen of Olympus and
patron of marriage and children, then Poseidon who
is directed to the seas and Hades who is sent to the
kingdom beneath the earth. On each occasion a pupil
is beckoned to his due position, as Zeus delivers a
running commentary which leaves the class in no
doubt about each one's name and status, 'And you
Hermes, with your winged heels and bright eyes, who
can circle the earth quicker than the speed of
light, you will be my messenger.' When the leading
gods are assembled, Zeus turns to the pupils who
have not left their places, 'And what of you mortals, earthlings, men and women, You may wonder how
we immortals came to inhabit Olympus and to rule you
below.' At this point the 'mortals' are invited to
question Zeus, and in the course of the interrogation he describes his own birth, the war against the
titans and introduces Prometheus and his brother.
To conclude the lesson, Zeus directs the class to
the text and asks them to read Chapter One. He
offers to come down from Olympus in order to answer
any queries they may have about its content.
     The teacher's objectives for the lesson which
follows are to help pupils to understand the significance of the Prometheus myth and to help them to
appreciate the two distinct viewpoints in the story.
The pupils, with one exception, are divided into
groups of four; they are told that they will represent lumps of clay. The lesson takes place in the
partially darkened hall and the teacher, as Zeus,
positions himself on the stage in a pool of light
while the class are seated below. Zeus beckons the
pupil who will play Prometheus and orders, 'Prometheus, you will make mortals out of clay and I will
breathe life into them.' The titan does as he is
told and, as the human forms emerge, Zeus bestows
life on them and they return to their groups to constitute families. The teacher comes out of role and
the pupils are sent back to their texts to read the
beginning of Chapter Three in their groups. Each
group is then asked to demonstrate, through drama,
the ignorance and vulnerability of man before Prometheus has taught them the skills and crafts of life
and bestowed on them the gift of fire. As Prometheus moves from group to group his influence
spreads and the mortals find the skills and the fire
that they so desperately need. The teacher, as
Zeus, suddenly cries from above, 'Titan, you have
disobeyed me! What is there to stop me casting you
into Tartarus with your brothers and destroying
these vile mortals to whom you have given fire,

which is reserved for the gods alone?' Prometheus, primed in advance, refuses to apologise for his action, and earns Zeus's anger and a terrible punishment. Pupils are then asked, out of role and in their groups, to decide why fire should have been of such significance to early man that it merited a myth of this sort. Finally, the groups are asked to put forward the arguments that Zeus might use in order to justify the denial of fire to mankind, and those Prometheus might put forward to justify the gift of fire to those he has created.

In the second example, a teacher of a similar group of twelve year old pupils wishes to demonstrate the need for myths to explain natural but apparently inexplicable phenomena. She begins by describing the life style of a primitive pre-Christian Greek race who lacked fire and the skills required to build houses and make tools. She asks the class to suggest questions and problems which would perplex such a people and which would seem to demand an answer. The teacher divides the class into groups of four, representing two parents and two children, or variations on this pattern, and presents them with a problem: The children, brighter than their parents, wish to know where they came from, how they were created and why they were put upon the earth. Given that they do not have recourse to a scientific explanation, the parents will need to find a suitably convincing story for their offspring. Once the parents have collaborated and decided on their 'myth', they recount this to their children, who are encouraged to ask as many questions as they wish. The groups share their myths with each other in a plenary session which ends the lesson.

At the beginning of the next lesson the teacher introduces a new problem through a question which the children will again ask of their parents, 'Why is there death and disease in the world - what have we done to deserve such hardships?' Only when pupils have devised their own answers to this and developed their own mythical framework, do they turn to the text to read the tales of Prometheus and Pandora. The pupil's understanding of these tales is demonstrated using the earlier format. The same two questions are asked but the parents now have different answers for their children, based on their reading of the text. The teacher concludes this sequence of work by asking, 'But what if your children say "Show us how it was, so that we can see it for ourselves"? How will you portray what actually happened?' The pupils, in groups, return to the text to select key moments in the first three chapters, which unfold the Prometheus and Pandora myths. Each group then chooses to focus on one incident which is developed and dramatised. The lesson ends with a class discussion which seeks to relate these Greek myths to twentieth century man's apparent need to create 'myths' of his own.

'The Diary of a Nobody'

George and Weedon Grossmith's 'The Diary of a Nobody'[4] is perhaps a less obvious choice as a class reader. In this example, the teacher of a class of able second year pupils favours it because of its anecdotal, informal style and as a nineteenth century contrast to the contemporary texts the class have studied, but one that does not pose any obvious problems in terms of obscurity of language. The teacher chooses it, well aware of its dramatic potential, having seen a successful BBC serialisation. He aims to contrast style and content with that of other diary writers, including the popular Kenneth Williams[5] and Adrian Mole[6].

As the class, divided into reading groups for the purpose, finish reading the first chapter of the text, the teacher asks them to look back over this in order to produce a cast list, as if for a play, accompanied by a brief description of each character. For example:

>   Willie Pooter: son to Charles and Carrie,
>   working in a bank in Oldham,
>   missed by his parents.

The pupils are then asked to select any moment, however slight, from the first chapter, which seems to suggest something of the relationship between Carrie and Charles Pooter. For example:

>   'April 5. Two shoulders of mutton arrived,
>   Carrie having arranged with another butcher
>   without consulting me.'

Using the information gained and deduced thus far about those involved, the groups are asked to discuss and decide what might have been said and done to prompt this diary entry, before explaining their interpretation to the rest of the class.

The class then returns to the text to read Chapter Two. The teacher asks the groups to focus on a more than usually eventful day in this section and to decide whether Charles Pooter's account of events represents the whole truth. Each group demonstrates its interpretation of the 'truth' through their dramatic enaction of the scene. This is ext-

ended in an improvised scene in which Charles describes that day's events to his wife and which explores Carrie's reactions. As the groups return to
read the next chapter, the teacher points out that
they are like the television adapter, the screenplay
writer, who must select from a text those parts
which are most suitable for inclusion in the dramatisation. As they read on he asks them to note
those scenes which would be worthy of incorporation
in an hour long television adaptation. Before
starting the task, the groups discuss the principles
which will decide which scenes will be included.
They suggest factors such as interest, overall contrast of mood, scenes which convey key information
or which explore central relationships in the book.
The teacher suggests that, as their extended piece
of work connected with the text, they might consider
the following:

> A description of those scenes which you would
> choose for dramatisation in an hour long tele-
> vision adaptation, with a commentary to justify
> your selection.

> A script to show what is said by the characters
> involved in such a scene, complete with stage
> directions.

> Directions for the designer of the television
> sets, describing the environment in which any
> one scene would take place.

> A description of a key scene through the eyes
> of an observant spectator, for example, Sarah
> the servant, Darwitts at the Mansion House
> Ball.

In the second example, a teacher of a third year
class of average ability has been trying to confront
the problem posed by pupils who devalue their own
experiences and feel that they lack sufficient interest in their own lives to fuel imaginative
writing. He collects a selection of 'A Life in the
Day of...' articles from the Sunday Times colour
magazine and distributes them to the class. Having
read and discussed the contents with a neighbour,
pupils are asked to describe the day to the rest of
the class. They then jot down in rough what happens
to them in the course of a fairly typical day, in
chronological sequence. The teacher asks them to
turn the light of hyperbole on this account, so that

a perfectly humdrum journey such as the walk from
home to school is seen in an extraordinary light.
That is, the events remain essentially the same but
the perception of the first person narrator is
changed, so that anyone reading the account in the
Sunday Times would be immediately intrigued. Pupils, working in fours, are asked to choose any one
of the days described by the group and to work out
the exaggerated interpretation dramatically.

At the beginning of the next lesson, in order
to counter the argument, 'We don't know enough about
anything to write about it', the teacher asks the
class to suggest all the areas in which they are
experts. They are, for example all experts in knowing what it feels like to be themselves in that
particular lesson at that particular time. No doctor and certainly no teacher knows more about how
it feels to be that body and mind, and what the individual says he or she thinks and registers cannot
be disputed. The teacher asks them to consider the
possibility that there may be more than one 'I',
that identity is not fixed but in a state of flux
which includes all the 'Is' which are projected in
order to meet what society, and particularly parents
and peer groups, seem to demand. Pupils then discuss, in groups, the nature of these demands and
the, sometimes conflicting, pressures they face. At
this point the teacher reads a section from 'The
Secret Diary of Adrian Mole' and asks, 'Has that, or
something similar, ever happened to you?' Once the
point has been made that Adrian Mole is not extraordinary, the teacher asks, 'Why is this interesting
even though the events are not extraordinary?' The
pupils come to the conclusion that interest is added
to everyday occurrences through the interesting nature of the perceiver, who presents them in a new
light. Pupils then choose either to write their own
entries for their own 'Secret Diaries', assuming a
new name and a different family, or move immediately
to a dramatisation of a possible entry. It is only
when these preliminaries are complete that the class
turns to 'The Diary of a Nobody'.

'The Guardians'
Many teachers of English feel that a single reader
is unlikely to interest and stimulate all the pupils in a class, particularly where the class is a
mixed ability one. One alternative is offered by
reading groups, which come closer to primary school
practice, where pupils choose, or are allocated to
groups and are allotted or choose their group

reader. In the example which follows, the teacher has selected seven different readers, which allows a modicum of choice since each group can elect to ignore one reader. She has six copies of each for distribution to her middle band second year class. Each of the six reading groups, containing five pupils, concentrates on their allotted text for approximately half a term. It is the spring term and pupils are already used to a system which sends them to workcards which describe suggestions for reading-related assignments. The teacher though is concerned to encourage pupils to negotiate their own assignments within the group and with the teacher, and asks each group to decide how the book will be most sensibly read. Every time a pupil makes a feasible suggestion he is asked to incorporate it in a new workcard which is filed with the teacher's initial 'core' assignments, thus increasing the choice of work for other groups who will, in turn, move on to the book in the course of the half termly cycle. There is a certain amount of 'spill over' space since the adjacent classroom is fortuitously empty on the Wednesday afternoons when these reading double periods take place and, when the weather is fine, the hall can be used.

The teacher is an admirer of John Christopher's work and has included 'The Guardians'[7] as one of the seven titles, since she hopes that, if it proves successful as a class reader, pupils may be encouraged to seek out his other books from the school library. The group of six pupils first use the information extracted from the front and back covers of the book, as they have been taught, in order to gain a general impression of its content. First impressions are aired orally. The group then makes some provisional decisions about how to approach the reading of the text. They are well aware of the options: each member of the group may read a section in turn, the whole text or parts may be read silently, and certain parts may be brought to life by reading only the direct speech. The group has learned, with some prompting from the teacher in the course of her perambulations, to interject relevant questions, 'When's it all happening?', 'What does "taciturn" mean?' Sometimes a scribe is nominated to jot down the answers to these questions as the reading continues. On occasions the group experiments with skipping short passages to gauge how much is lost. When important points have been missed, the teacher redirects attention with a well-placed question. Groups are allowed to read the books

intensively or may intersperse the reading with
self-chosen tasks. They may choose to attack these
tasks as a group, as sub-groups, pairs or individuals, since different assignments will demand different approaches.

The group has chosen to read 'The Guardians'
intensively, perhaps unsurprisingly, since the narrative moves at a rapid pace. It describes how Rob
escapes from the sterile world of the Conurb in the
year 2050 to the County beyond, where he is adopted
by the affluent Gifford family. Rob is forced to
decide whether he will side with his adoptive parents and those content with their comfortable lot,
or with those revolutionaries who determine to fight
with their comrades in the Conurb. Once they have
finished reading the book, the group turns to the
worksheet which the teacher devised at the beginning
of the year but which has, by this point, been
supplemented by pupil suggestions:

'The Guardians'. Choose any three of these assignments. You may work on them on your own, as a pair
or as a group, but you must record your answers
individually.

1. Which questions are posed in this book and
   not answered until near the end? Are there
   any questions which are posed but never
   fully answered?
2. Are you convinced that by the year 2050
   English society will have changed to this
   extent? Give reasons for your answers.
3. What do we mean when we say that a character in a book, programme or film is a
   'sympathetic' one? Did you find Rob a
   sympathetic character in all parts of the
   book?
4. Imagine you are going to dramatise this
   book as a three part serial for children's
   television.
   In general terms, what kinds of scenes are
   you likely to select and include? Specifically, which scenes will you include?
   Imagine you are the director: Select a
   scene and describe as fully as possible the
   directions you would give the actors taking
   part in it.
5. If we could invite the author in to talk to
   us about the book what questions would you
   wish to put to him? What answers do you
   think John Christopher might give you?

6. Why do you think John Christopher pays particular attention to Rob's books in 'The Guardians'?
Do you think books are threatened in the 1980s? If so, by whom or what? What do we mean by 'literacy' and 'numeracy'? Do you think it is more important to be literate - or numerate today?

Self-chosen or suggested assignments: To be developed in pairs or as a group. Please make sure you discuss your choice with your teacher. This book raises many interesting issues which you might like to explore through drama:

A. You might like to look <u>back</u> in time, eg to the first meeting and courtship of Rob's parents in Shearam, Gloucestershire or <u>forward</u> in time to the eventual meeting between Rob and Mike at the Southampton Conurb. Both meetings would, in their different ways, be dangerous.

B. You might present a debate, where one speaker presents the views of Sir Percy Gregory and another presents the views of Mike Gifford. Can you think of any circumstances in which the two might be brought together in order to defend their views? (There are other characters in the book whose opinions might be contrasted.)

C. You might like to present a different view of English society in 2050 and consider changes in the way the country is governed, in education, transport, housing, family relationships, eating habits, dress etc.

While answering question two, one group hits upon the idea of representing, through drama, the important meeting of revolutionaries which takes place in the Kennealys' apartment, early in the book and which is only dimly perceived by Rob. They begin by discussing and then describing the course of the meeting; this forms the basis for the improvisation which takes place at their desks, since the cramped conditions of the classroom seem to provide the most appropriate location for the scene. Their suggestion is finally added to the end of the assignment sheet.

Another group picks out a particularly vivid moment in Rob's last conversation with his adoptive Aunt Margaret, when he attempts to persuade her that

her son's flight to freedom is preferable to the
'operation on his brain, to stop him being rebell-
ious, make him docile.' She replies, 'I believe
you. It is something that can't be helped. There
is a scar on my husband's head; his hair hides it.
It happened when he was a young man, before we were
married.' The teacher asks the group, 'Do you think
such a thing - or similar things - could be happening today?' The pupils are unsure and spend what
remains of the lesson discussing the issue. The
teacher appears at the beginning of the next lesson
with a number of newspaper cuttings. One describes
a report which claims that Richard Nixon went to
extraordinary underhand lengths to implicate John
Lennon because of his supposed influence on young
people, another describes the advances in the development of laser weapons, designed to destroy nuclear
arms and a third reports on a freak medical operation in which the head of one animal was sewn on to
the body of another. The teacher suggests that the
group might begin to collect their own portents of
a world to come and might include them in their work
folder. Out of the discussion which is stimulated
by these disconcerting newspaper extracts, come
suggestions which lead into associated drama work,
'They sometimes make mistakes in operations - What
if you went in for an ordinary operation and came
out with your brain reprogrammed?', 'What if you
began to speak out and were sent into space, going
round and round for ever, or out of our universe and
into another one?' The teacher makes the point
that, in a way, this is what is happening in Rob's
world when prisoners are sent to fight in the war in
China. She then asks, 'If you were all powerful - a
totalitarian ruler in a state without books - and
you wanted to influence and dominate people's minds,
how would you do it?' The pupils suggest, 'Through
television, through holovision.' This prompts consideration of the role of holovision in the Conurb,
and the entire group finally decides to show how a
holovision magazine programme might reflect the
views of the government and the nature of society in
the Conurb in the year 2050. They take as their
starting point the riot which follows the Games
session, described at the beginning of the book, and
discuss how this might be presented, contrasting
this with its nearest 1980s equivalent, the football
riot. The group chooses to use the familiar television magazine devices, the studio anchor man and
commentator, the outside broadcast interview and the
studio discussion group. This work generates its

own suggestions for further assignments, a transcription of the interviews, a science examination
paper for the year 2050 and an entry for a history
book of 2100, describing these riots in retrospect.

THE EXAMINATION SET TEXT

Drama has a particularly significant contribution to
make to the study of texts prescribed by the C.S.E.,
16+, 'O' and 'A' Level syllabus. Here, concentration on a relatively small number of examination
texts may encourage detailed analysis but, in so
doing, may lead to horribly narrow and tedious study
methods. These are epitomised by an obsessive cram-
ming where meaning and enjoyment are destroyed in
the interests of rehearsed answers to examination
questions. There is a particular need, in the
examination years, to return the initiative to the
students and to help them, on Piagetian lines, to
assimilate and accommodate the material in their own
terms. In drama the students' contributions are all
important, since it demands that participants think
through the implications of statements, actions and
options, for themselves. The examples of work which
follow aim, despite the references to specific age
groups, to display general approaches to English and
drama which cross the C.S.E., 16+, 'O' and 'A' Level
divide.

'The Bees Have Stopped Working and Other Stories'

The class of fifteen year old C.S.E. students have
been reading this collection[8] of Bill Naughton's
short stories as part of their course work. Any
written work stimulated by the text will form part
of their formally examined C.S.E. literature folders. The teacher is very much aware that if he is
not careful the reading of the anthology will become
a rather solitary, routine affair as students plod
from one story to the next. Thus, before launching
the class into the stories, he notes those scenes
which invite pair and group work, and oral and drama
work. The class has done little or no educational
drama since their first year and the teacher is
eager to move them towards classroom drama, however
modest this may be.
    He begins by reading aloud one of the collec-
tion, 'Seeing a Beauty Queen Home', which has obvious dramatic potential. This first person narrative describes how an arrogant young man, fancying
his chances, escorts Maggie, the Cotton Town Beauty
Queen, home only to be met by her formidable Gran.

He craftily and successfully passes himself off as
Ernie Adams, a young man whom Gran respects, but in
the process convinces Maggie that he is too smart
for his, and her, own good and earns a miserable
walk home. The teacher sees script work as an appropriate and accessible route into classroom drama
and, significantly, an approach which is popular
with the students. They are asked, working in small
groups, to adapt the story as if for performance as
a radio play. In the course of preliminary discussion, the students decide that they will have to represent those thoughts of the narrator which are
needed to make the story intelligible, and will have
to pay particular attention to the way lines are
spoken, since texture of voice will be important in
a story in which the main characters are hiding
behind a screen of deception, for at least part of
the time. The teacher asks each group to consider
how they will differentiate between the narrator's
thoughts and his speech. Each group begins to analyse the story, section by section, jotting down
their suggestions describing how lines should be
spoken. These jottings form the basis for a final
annotated version. Once they are happy with a section, the students try it out aloud. They have
access to a pair of tape recorders in order to gauge
the effect of their interpretation. In this way the
teacher hopes to fulfil his three objectives, to
find a more stimulating approach to reading and comprehension, to highlight the importance of voice
type and tone in revealing personality, and, through
asking students to contract the narrative for the
purposes of their adaptations, to provide a more
meaningful context for summary work.
    Each group is eager to tape the final inter-
pretation for performance and for comparison with
those of the rest of the class, and this modest
approach to drama has the desired effect since students are enthusiastic to extend this approach to
other stories. A group of boys reads 'Weaver's
Knot' from the same collection; it tells of a novice
weaver's touching concern for the older woman who
supervises his work in the weaving shed and who
eventually loses her baby, fathered by the apparently coarse overlooker, Eddie. The group objects,
'It's soft Sir. He wouldn't feel like it says about
the baby, he's too innocent.' The teacher asks,
'Are you saying it's too sentimental?' One of the
group replies, 'Well it starts alright, but then it
doesn't seem true.' The teacher asks them to define
the point at which they feel the story takes an un-

convincing turn and to 'rewrite' the story from that
point, through drama. He suggests they begin by
discussing the possible options for moving the story
forward, before focussing on one or more to see how
they might work as dramatic improvisations. The
important place of work, or lack of it, in these
stories prompts another group to look at the 'jar-
gon' associated with the different kinds of work
portrayed in these stories and to explore, through
drama, the differences between the management's,
unions' and workforce's use of language. They do
this through reference to a local, but nationally
reported, industrial dispute where their dramatic
exploration of the possible background to the strike
is presented convincingly in the classroom as a
series of meetings, involving all sectors of the
management and workforce and ending with a realistic
news conference.

'The Nun's Priest's Tale'

This group of 'A' Level English students are about
to move from a general 'pick and mix' survey of
English literature to the first of their examination
set texts, 'The Nun's Priest's Tale', at the beginning of the Spring Term of their Lower Sixth year.
The teacher realises that the class is approaching
Chaucer with some trepidation since they have only
met 'The Canterbury Tales', if at all, in modern
translations and are intimidated by Chaucer's reputation for being archaic and obscure. The teacher,
too, is not looking forward to the routine paraphrase which can involve too much teacher explanation and much passive note-making on the part of
students. She wants to give the paraphrase some
purpose, apart from the rather frightening demands
of the 'gobbet' examination questions, and hits upon
the idea of translating the tale for performance to
a class of top juniors in the primary school which
shares the school's site. Thus she wishes to share
the responsibility for making Chaucer's words spring
to life with her students and hopes that, together,
they will reveal the universal appeal of the tale
and its theme. More particularly, she wishes to
bolster liaison between the senior and junior
school, by showing sixth formers and secondary
school English in an interesting and accessible
light. It is hoped that the whole process will
reveal Chaucer as an inspired wordsmith and maker of
tales and will place this tale in its true setting
as oral narrative, rather than merely page-bound
poem. The junior school teacher concerned is eager

to exploit the project and invites the Lower Six
group in during school hours, to meet their future
audience and to introduce the story to the class,
thus breaking the ice all round and allowing the
junior school pupils opportunities for associated
art work and imaginative writing.

The examination rubric makes it quite clear
that any paraphrase of the original should be into
clear, intelligible, modern English prose and the
teacher suggests to the Lower Six students that this
will be the rule for the dramatisation, since it
should make sense to the average ten to eleven year
old. The class decides that the best way of setting
about the paraphrase is to divide it into sections,
making a pair of students responsible for each unit.
The teacher acts as consultant on the occasions when
the students' inspired guess work and textual notes
fail them. Once each pair and the teacher are happy
with their interpretations, these are compared, in
order to produce a uniformity of style. The whole
is then typed by two of the class, as secretarial
practice, before being duplicated and distributed.

One period is put aside at the end of Thursday
afternoons for making the production decisions which
follow. Where extra time is needed the class and
teacher continue working after four o'clock. The
students decide which parts of the original will be
deleted or summarised and which parts will be elaborated through action, to reinforce their dramatic
impact. They decide that a narrator, the Nun's
Priest, is a necessity but that any direct speech
will be delivered by the animal concerned, whether
the fox, Chaunticleer the cockerel, or Pertelote the
hen. At this point the teacher suggests that they
make lists for each of the main characters, using
the headings 'Appearance' and 'Personality', since
a dramatic interpretation will only be possible if
the class has grasped the characteristics of the
creatures they aim to portray. In the interests of
future essay writing, students are asked to quote
the sources for their conclusions, which are then
shared with the rest of the class. They are well
aware that Chaunticleer is both a cockerel and a
quasi courtly figure and that Pertelote is both the
gracious and elegant woman of the world and a lowly
hen. The fox is the archetypal crafty villain but
even he has sufficient vision to recognise his own
folly. Since the animals are such subtle anthropo-
morphic creations, the students are concerned about
how to distinguish between the animals and humans in
the minds of their young audience. Somewhat facet-

iously, one of the class suggests, 'How about putting the animals on roller skates?' This suggestion
is accepted enthusiastically as a novel solution.
Costume proves to pose less of a problem since one
of the students takes up the challenge as an art
project and, with the help of the art department,
produces some excellent papier mâché combs for
Chaunticleer and his hens. Bright blue lurex leg
warmers provide Chaunticleer with 'his legges' 'lyk
asure' and he sports a magnificent many-layered
gold foil cape. The chic Pertelote has a diaphanous
costume which she swishes to great effect when she
suspects Chaunticleer of cowardice. The fox has a
moulded papier mâché mask from which he can peep, in
order to convey to the audience his true villainous
intentions.

The performance takes place out of doors in
June, after the Lower Sixth summer examinations, in
the junior school playground, using an old garden
shed for the poor widow's 'narwe cotage'. At the
moment when Chaunticleer is dragged away by the fox,
the entire cast circle the cottage in a flurry of
feathers and cries of alarm. The project is sufficiently successful to inspire a similar one in the
following year when the current Lower Six 'A' Level
group dramatise Chaucer's 'The Pardoner's Tale' for
performance to a first year secondary school audience in the lunch hour. In both cases both adapters
and audience benefit: for the sixth formers the
words become fact through costume and action, making
the obscure meaningful and memorable, and the performance inspires creative reverberations in English
and drama work in the first year.

'Macbeth'

If 'O' and 'A' Level students find Chaucer difficult
then Shakespeare's plays can seem doubly so. Like
Chaucer's Middle English, the unfamiliarity and density of Shakespeare's blank verse are a barrier to
understanding, but here the depth of the imagery can
cause even more problems of interpretation. Too
often students see Shakespeare's plays more as narrative prose, even as novels, rather than as blue-
prints for actual performance. They will be helped
to see his plays in a more realistic light if they
are made aware of the way the 1623 Folio came into
being, as the later record of live commercial performance, tentative in parts, and introducing act
divisions where they were scarcely necessary in performance. Students should be helped to move away
from the habitual theme spotting which can bedevil

any real understanding of the primary human concerns
of the characters, to a negotiation of meaning which
can only take place when the words are let loose
from the page, in space and time and feeling.

'Macbeth' is a favourite 'O' and 'A' Level set
text, put crudely because it is short, 'meaty' in
its speed of action and in its obsession with evil,
and because it spawns the sort of examination questions favoured by examiners and familiar to all
teachers of English:

> Macbeth - Man or Monster? Discuss.
> 'Macbeth is not ruined by others but through
> his own free will.' Illustrate.
> Examine the importance of the relationship
> between Lady Macbeth and Macbeth in deciding
> the course of events in the play.

One significant way of arriving at the answers to
such questions is through drama. Drama can make the
point that where problems of interpretation arise it
is often because there is no single right answer;
there is only the carefully justified interpretation, versus the shallow and spurious one. Drama's
concern here is with process rather than with performance, with what the protagonists feel and think
rather than with a single polished version, such as
that demanded by the school play. The outline which
follows describes one possible way in which drama as
process can help to transfer some of the responsibility for discovering meaning from the teacher to
students:

We might first select those scenes or speeches
which pose most questions, present most problems or
which are most important in deciding what follows,
and which do all three, since all three qualities
characterise key scenes in Macbeth. These include:
Act One, Scene Seven; Act Two, Scene One; Act Two,
Scene Two; Act Three, Scene Four; Act Five, Scene
Five. The play will first be read as quickly as
possible in order to grasp the course of the action
and the roles of the main protagonists. Television,
radio or film interpretations will supplement this
initial reading. Thus, as the class approaches the
first of these key scenes they will already have an
overview of the play and will be in a position to
see the scenes as part of the whole, as 'contextual'
areas which must be related to what precedes and
follows.

<u>Act One, Scene Seven</u>. Before launching into any

scene with a class, the teacher must first map out
for himself the areas for interpretation, and the
questions which need answering. The teacher's notes
for Act One, Scene Seven might read:

- a. Significance of stage directions which open
  scene: reference to 'Sewer and divers
  Servants'. Macbeth has deserted the feast.
- b. Juxtaposition of Macbeth's speech (1-28)
  with Duncan's gracious greeting (I.6).
- c. Establish the point Macbeth has reached by
  the end of soliloquy. Movement, both physical and emotional in this speech.

The teacher might, at this point, use the preceding events as a launching point for the analysis
which will follow. 'The Facts So Far' can be established through discussion and displayed most conveniently on an overhead projector:

Act One, Scene One: Three witches, malevolent
in intention, will meet Macbeth on the heath.
Act One, Scene Two: Macbeth is a great general
and loyal to his king. He has won two major
and bloody battles.
Act One, Scene Three: The witches foretell
that Macbeth will be Thane of Cawdor and 'king
hereafter'. Banquo will only beget kings.
Macbeth, accepting the title of Thane of Cawdor
from Duncan, begins to believe in the witches'
prophecies, but his belief unsettles him.
Act One, Scene Four: Macbeth reaffirms his
loyalty. Duncan makes Malcolm his heir and
Macbeth recognises that this conferment ob-
structs his path to kingship. Duncan will stay
with Macbeth at Inverness.
Act One, Scene Five: Lady Macbeth receives
news from Macbeth of the witches' prophecies
and immediately fears that Macbeth's humanity
will quell his determination. She broaches
this with Macbeth who does not commit himself.
Act One, Scene Six: Lady Macbeth welcomes
Duncan to Inverness Castle.

After the students have had a chance to reread
Act One, Scene Seven silently, the teacher might
begin by establishing the objective for the lesson,
'To answer the question - Why does Macbeth decide to
murder Duncan?' In attempting to arrive at an answer, the class will inevitably look beyond Act One,
Scene Seven to the scenes which follow it. The

teacher might then point out that in the course of
fifty lines in this scene, Macbeth has moved from
'We will proceed no further in this business' to 'I
am settled; and bend up/Each corporal agent to this
terrible feat' and that before this scene little is
known of the relationship between Macbeth and Lady
Macbeth. At this point two students can read from
line thirty one to the end of the scene, without
preamble, but as expressively as possible. We might
then ask, 'What do we now know about Macbeth and
Lady Macbeth that the words on the page alone did
not tell us?' Students might then supplement this
initial interpretation, however wooden, with other
possibilities, for example:

a. Macbeth may be a courageous general but his
   wife dominates him in her own domestic
   sphere. She is eager for power for her own
   sake.
b. Macbeth is resolute in all things; it is
   only this drastic step which makes him
   vacillate. It takes his wife whom he respects and loves to spur him to action.
c. Lady Macbeth is eager for power for Macbeth
   because she loves him and feels it is his
   due. The power of her arguments, rather
   than the strength of their relationship and
   the witches' prophecies, tip Macbeth into
   murder.

This list is not of course exhaustive. We might
then invite the class to adopt hypotheses and to reread the scene in pairs, with their chosen hypothesis in mind in order to gauge the effect in practice. The students will need to pay particular
attention to key words and phrases, which they
should be able to select for themselves. Opinions
may vary and different interpretations will determine which these will be. We might, for example,
ask students to decide how many ways the following
could conceivably be said:

Line 31: We will proceed no further in this
business.
Lines 38-39: From this time/Such I account thy
love.
Line 45: Prithee peace.
Line 59: Macbeth   If we should fail
          Lady   We fail!

Here the Folio gives Lady Macbeth's answer a question mark, though this is ambiguous and an exclamation mark is favoured by some scholars. Students might explore the impact each has on the meaning here.

There is no need for students to perform in front of each other necessarily; the important thing is that they should be forced into a position where they must articulate their interpretation of the scene. It is this articulation and the discussion and justification which accompany it which are most valuable. If students have not already plotted their speeches in space, they should consider the implications of their interpretation for movement and gesture. For those students who do not take to this naturally, a few questions may stimulate thought:

> Do Lady Macbeth and Macbeth look directly at each other throughout this scene?
> Does either dominate the audience's attention at the front of the stage? If so, when?
> Does either touch the other? How? Why? Where? Does it receive a response? (Almost any sort of touch, embrace and blow is possible within the emotional parameters of this scene, though some are inevitably more likely than others.)
> How do the characters enter? Exit?

There are, of course, many other ways of approaching this scene. This method works from hypothesis to text; a more open approach might, equally justifiably, take the students from text to hypothesis.

Act Two, Scene One, Lines 33-64. This speech may, if the students have sufficient understanding of the adjoining scenes, be presented alone, divorced from the text, as an informal contextual question. In this case, the teacher might begin by asking, 'Macbeth is alone. Who has just left the scene?' After an initial reading aloud, again to get a feel of the words, the class might discuss the particular problems this speech poses for an actor, because it is a soliloquy and because of the nature of the speech, (since Macbeth follows an imaginary dagger which seems to lead him to Duncan's chamber). The class, working in pairs, might then consider the structure of the speech as a preliminary to determining their own dramatic interpretation and in order to make the speech more manageable from an actor's point of view. They might begin by dividing

the speech into two, justifying their division, then
move on to dividing it into three and thence four,
on each occasion discussing their decisions with the
rest of the class in order to see how these reflect
their interpretation of the movement of tone and
pace in the speech. Students might proceed to mark
up their scripts, indicating those words and phrases
which demand particular attention (for example, the
last three lines) and those parts of the speech
which, in the light of the previous exercise, seem
to require a quickening or a slackening of pace,
volume or tone. Finally, one student might deliver
the speech while the other directs his movements
throughout, in order to lend meaning and momentum to
what is said. Thus, the layers of meaning are built
up in stages.

<u>Act Two, Scene Two</u>. It is possible to work on this
scene as a whole, but I prefer to work more intensively on one possible 'movement' in the scene, from
the beginning, to the moment when Lady Macbeth recognises the presence of the incriminating daggers.
By this stage, students should be able to ask their
own questions of the text and to pick out the most
telling words and phrases. There are many questions
which might be asked of this scene, including:

a. Is it possible to read the first speech of
   Lady Macbeth as though she was the imper-
   viously wicked queen of fairy tale?
b. What is Shakespeare doing when he includes
   the word 'afraid' in her next speech, and
   chooses to tell us that if it were not for
   Duncan's resemblance to her father she
   would have committed the murder?
c. <u>How</u> is Macbeth carrying the 'two blood-
   stained daggers'?
d. Why does Lady Macbeth greet Macbeth with
   the words 'My husband!', rather than the
   more formal appellation used at I. 5. 52?
e. Why should Lady Macbeth apparently ignore
   the bizarre and incriminating sight of the
   two daggers until line 48?
f. What does the stychomythic disjunction of
   lines 16-19 suggest about the states of
   mind of the speakers at this point? What
   is happening to Macbeth in the course of
   these speeches?
g. Is Macbeth addressing Lady Macbeth in his
   speeches, lines 22-43, or is he talking to
   himself?

    h.   Does Lady Macbeth believe that Macbeth's anxieties are barely worth consideration or is this simply a ploy to cut through Macbeth's ominous thoughts? Is she truly impervious to guilt and the implications of the murder, as she exits to fabricate the evidence?

The class might begin by answering these or similar questions, before taking to their feet to incorporate their answers in their reading of the text. They might equally well start with the text, arriving at their answers on their feet, reacting to the impact of the other voice and presence. Thus, put at its simplest, Lady Macbeth may find herself infected with Macbeth's fear, or reacting against it; she may respond with anger to his insular deliberations at one moment and yet try to rush him out of them, nurse-like, at another. Students may wish to focus on a kernal in the scene and work out from there, for example, from Macbeth's entrance with the daggers to Lady Macbeth's 'A foolish thought, to say a sorry sight.' In pairs, they might look at questions of tone, volume, bodily proximity and all the other paralinguistic means of communication, in this short section. They will need to look below the ambiguity and apparent irrelevance of some of the speakers' words to delve for the meanings beneath. Some students may opt to focus on Macbeth, standing for speech after speech with two blood-stained daggers in his hands, and answer the question, 'What effect does the presence of the daggers have on the way Macbeth is thinking, speaking and moving?'

Act Three, Scene Four. It is difficult, without trying it out, to visualise the banqueting arrangements for this scene and thus it is difficult to realise how far and how fast the scene moves from apparent unity and order to the disturbance and disorder of the end. One way of approaching this issue is through the eyes of the stage manager or director, visualising the scene diagramatically. Students might begin by asking,

Single table or many tables, or are such props superfluous?

How and where do Lady Macbeth and Macbeth enter at the beginning of the scene?

Where does Lady Macbeth sit - is she on the

same level as the assembled lords?

Why and how does Macbeth walk 'around the tables'?

Where does he sit?

Where does he encounter the First Murderer?

Is his conversation with the First Murderer a static affair or is some stage business indicated between the speeches?

Is Macbeth in full view of Lady Macbeth when she reminds him of his responsibilities as host?

Where exactly is Macbeth when the ghost of Banquo takes his seat?

What movements take Macbeth from this point to the realisation of the ghost's presence?

Where, in her speech, and in the hall, does Lady Macbeth meet Macbeth to ask 'Are you a man?'

What movements accompany Lady Macbeth's speech beginning, 'O proper stuff!'?

and so forth, through the scene to the final moments where Macbeth and Lady Macbeth remain alone, drained and despairing, Macbeth resolutely preparing for further crimes and Lady Macbeth already on the path to sleep walking and suicide.

All these questions can be answered in an annotated diagram. This is not a frivolous or irrelevant exercise since it starts the search for meaning in the relationship between words and movement. Different directorial diagrams will reveal how much scope there is in this scene for many interpretive patterns of movement. The exercise should also reveal the contrasts in the scene, between rule and misrule, truth and hypocrisy, movement and stillness, the public and private space, the public and private voice, darkness and light and sanity and madness. At least one of the interpretations should be worked through, once the participating group is aware of the director's requirements. At this point attention can turn to the words and, in particular, to the pacing of Macbeth's speeches, and to finding

the voices for his dramatic switches from hospitable
tyrant to vulnerable assassin.

Act Five, Scene Five, Lines 17-28. Macbeth is
numbed by horror and immune to pity as Act Five,
Scene Five begins. He is besieged by Malcolm's
soldiers without, and by his own past within, and is
too far gone in crime to feel the impact of Lady
Macbeth's death, which he uses to suggest the futil-
ity of human existence. The speech beginning, 'She
should have died hereafter' is a particularly telling and powerful one and its significance will evap-
orate if it is merely read at a desk. It is a
speech which causes particular problems for 'O' and
'A' Level students, in part because it is often so
badly read and because of the density of the imagery. Students need to hear, ideally see, the speech
performed by professional actors. They should know
of Ian McKellen's understanding of the soliloquy[9]:

> So, if we take a speech like Macbeth's last
> soliloquy 'Tomorrow and tomorrow and tomorrow'
> which, to crudely summarise, is a description
> of total blackness, total despair, that life is
> finite, it isn't enough just to put despair
> into the voice and follow the rhythms. You've
> got to do many more things as well. You have
> to think and have analysed in rehearsal tot-
> ally, so that your imagination being fed by the
> concrete metaphors, concrete images, pictures,
> can then feed through into the body, into ges-
> ture, into timbre of voice, into eyelids, into
> every part of the actor's make up, so that it
> does seem that he is making it up as he goes
> along, although he knows that he isn't...
> 'Tomorrow and tomorrow and tomorrow and tomor-
> row and tomorrow...'
> What does that word mean - tomorrow. It's beg-
> inning to have the lack of meaning I think that
> Macbeth detects in his own life at this point.
> 'Creeps in this petty pace from day to day.'
> And here comes the first metaphor, the first
> image, and the rhythm is beginning to creep, is
> beginning to plod, like someone plodding along
> a country lane. It's footsteps now. Not the
> tick-tock of a clock...
> 'And our yesterdays have lighted fools/The way
> to dusty death.'
> What is the image there that I must have clear-
> ly in my mind so that I can get the right emo-
> tion of despair? It's what? It's a fool walk-

ing along a dusty path, plodding, creeping with petty pace...A village idiot wandering along a country lane with what? A guttering candle? I don't know. A lantern?...
'Out, out, brief candle!'
The fool's candle has caught a gust of wind and is blown out and he collapses into a dusty death in the unmade road of Elizabethan England. The last candle or light we see in the play is Lady Macbeth's candle, which she was carrying in her sleepwalking scene, and she is dead. It's Lady Macbeth's death; village idiot's death; it's going to be Macbeth's death; it's going to be everybody's death...One could say so much about it, but just let me run through the last words of each line and you'll see that they add up to what the speech is all about. Hereafter - word - tomorrow - today - time - fools - candle - player - stage - tale - fury - nothing.

McKellen's approach is inspiring in its enthusiasm, which never slips into pretentiousness or sycophancy, and in its insistence on Shakespeare's concrete, even homely, delineation of life, death and humanity. McKellen focusses on the reverberations set up by the patterning of words which, in their juxtaposition, produce more complex layers of meaning which can only emerge when the soliloquy is lifted from the page. As with Blake's 'Songs of Experience', students will first need to recognise that for all its deceptively simple lexis the meaning will not come glibly to hand; they will need to arrive at a provisional understanding before embarking on performance, however informal. As McKellen suggests, an understanding of the imagery should feed and fuel gesture and movement, and, as he puts it, 'I believe that if you look after the sense, the sounds will look after themselves.'

The exercises above are not exclusive to Macbeth but are intended as paradigms for approaches to many of Shakespeare's plays. Throughout, they keep close to the text and many will feel that this is the most sensible method when preparing students for a formal 'O' and 'A' Level literature examination. We might also approach the play through issues and themes, having discussed with the class what these might be: The corrosive effects of love, greed and conscience; the precarious dividing line between the socially condoned killing and murder, and between madness and obsession; the importance of convention

in the ordering of human affairs; the dangers of
dallying with the supernatural and occult; the mis-
use of power; the all pervasive nature of evil, and
so forth. All of these themes are as topical today
as they were in eleventh century Scotland or in
James the First's London, and can be explored dramatically through their twentieth century manifestations[10], so long as we are aware of the dangers of
giving the impression that Macbeth is little more
than a moralistic tract, a string of themes, spouted
through the mouths of automatons. For Macbeth is
supremely about human beings whom we can believe in,
who feel, suffer and have free will, and it is
through drama that this essential humanity will be
revealed.

NOTES

1. Jane Doonan, Ready Readers, Times Educational Supplement (18 February 1983).
2. Tom Stabler, Drama in Primary Schools,
Schools Council Drama 5-11 Project (Macmillan,
1978).
3. Roger Lancelyn Green, Tales of the Greek
Heroes (Penguin (Puffin), 1958).
4. George and Weedon Grossmith, The Diary of a
Nobody (Penguin, 1892).
5. Kenneth Williams, Back Drops: Pages from a
Private Diary (M. Dent & Sons, 1983).
6. Sue Townsend, The Secret Diary of Adrian
Mole aged 13¾ (Methuen, 1982).
7. John Christopher, The Guardians (Penguin,
1970).
8. Bill Naughton, The Bees Have Stopped Working and Other Stories (Wheaton, 1976).
9. See: The English Programme booklet 1981-
1982 (an extract from London Weekend Television's
The South Bank Show).
10. See, for example, Richard Adams and Gerard
Gould, Into Shakespeare, An Introduction to Shakespeare through Drama (Ward Lock, 1977).

Chapter Six

DRAMA AND THE ENGLISH THEME

Given the nature of 'English' as a curricular area,
it is not surprising to find that so many teachers
of English organise their work around a theme of one
sort or another. English can lack the structure and
rationale of a more linear subject such as mathemat-
ics or history and can appear rather fragmented and
inconsequential if a framework is not imposed to
discipline its breadth. The theme offers such a
framework, which is tight enough to impart coherence
and cohesion, yet loose enough to allow scope for
choice, initiative and creativity, key considera-
tions for the teacher of English and drama.
     Where themes for English and drama are concern-
ed, we might justifiably suggest, in the words from
the song, 'It ain't what you do, it's the way that
you do it', since almost any theme will work given
good will, careful organisation and ample stimuli
and choice. Even potentially controversial topics,
such as sex, death, and discrimination, which teachers tend to fight shy of, sometimes with good reason, can work if they are approached sensitively
with the needs, interests and maturity of the pupils
in mind. Most teachers of English though play safe,
choosing to develop the most popular themes, which
include: The Supernatural, Man and Machines, Crime
and Punishment, School, War, The Sea, Myths and
Legends, The Five Senses, Exploration. These titles
are reinforced by those suggested in course books.
'Mainspring English' 1 and 2[1], for example, offers:
Creepy Creatures, Childhood and School, Seasons,
Language, Town and City Life, Leisure, Food and
Drink, and Writers and Writing, as themes. 'Out-
look'[2] offers, among others: Family, School, Work,
Love, Sport, Heroes, Faces of War, and Into Space.
Such themes are sufficiently all-embracing to suit
almost any age group, and all will allow ample scope

for drama work.

Although course books and anthologies can be helpful, when used sparingly and carefully, they seldom alone fit the classroom bill, even given the excellence of some on the market[3]. Enlightened teachers of English will recognise that, since these books usually represent a single compiler's taste, they are unlikely to stimulate thirty distinct individuals in a typical class, which, even where it is supposedly homogeneous in ability, will hardly be homogeneous in its tastes. The repeated appearance of the course book makes English teaching seem all too predictable; 'Not that again' pupils are heard to mutter as they plod inexorably through its sections. We owe it to our pupils to surprise them, to allow them opportunities to develop their own ideas, rather than endlessly responding to the course book's suggestion for 'Follow Up Work'.

The danger with the theme of course is that of overkill. While we will not worry when the knowing second year pupil insists, 'We did that in top juniors, Sir', there is a danger of allowing the once new-minted theme to extend into tedium and boredom. This is all the more likely when themes are 'centralised' by the Head of English who requires that his staff continue with a theme, come hell and insubordination for the prescribed half term, without offering support and resources. Junior school teachers who use teacher directed topics but also allow themes to emerge and encourage pupils to devise their own, have got the balance right and often have a great deal to teach their secondary school colleagues who wade indiscriminately into the next of the course book's sections, without planning. Some themes are best suited to an intensive, whole class, short burst approach[4], others may be initiated by a single pupil or pair or group, and continue throughout the term, even, given sufficient commitment, throughout the year, fuelling a coursework folder or personal anthology. There is no reason why certain pupils, given permission, should not declare U.D.I. and pursue a theme of their own.

Well before broaching a theme we will need to consider possible approaches, including the balance between English and drama. Though some would rightly maintain that these two are indivisible, we will need to map out the kinds of drama experiences we have in mind: Is it a theme which encourages whole class drama work? Should we opt for a theme which lends itself to more sedentary classroom drama? The resources, space and time available will inevitably be decisive factors at the planning stage.

A single theme will allow several approaches, even where it is teacher-directed. Take 'Conflict' as a popular example. Here, initial jottings will immediately suggest the scope for development:

CONFLICT: Past - Present - Future

	'Reality', eg	'Literature', eg
Debate	The Family	Noah's Ark
Disagreement	Neighbours	Beowulf
Argument	At Work	Romeo and Juliet
Fighting	In History	A Poison Tree
War	In the Future	

The subdivision need not end here; the teacher or pupils may choose a subtheme and further divide it, thus:

CONFLICT: At Work: Management versus unions
Union versus union
Foreman versus worker
Worker versus worker
Staff versus clients: Guard
versus passenger: The Lost
Ticket

CONFLICT: In Literature: Beowulf
The dispute with Unferth
The fight with Grendel
The fight with Grendel's mother

This process of subdivision is similar in kind to Dorothy Heathcote's 'segmenting':

> She begins with a two-step process. First, she very quickly thinks of all the various aspects of the chosen subject that she can. This she typically does in her head, not with the class ...Heathcote's second step is to take one of the segments and, through questions, to arrive at a particular moment when the essence of that experience is likely to be the most fully recognised. The questions she poses lead the class to the moment of beginning...Heathcote has found it helpful...to think of those areas into which any culture may be divided...commerce, communication, clothing, education, family, food, health, law, leisure, shelter, travel, war, work, and worship.[5]

The fact that we will need to subdivide any theme for ourselves, in advance of classroom work, does not mean that these subdivisions will be imposed on the class. Rather, with the possibilities clear in our own minds, we will hope to manoeuvre pupils into suggesting their own interpretations and options. 'Conflict', as presented above, falls into two general sections, 'Reality' and 'Literature'. These two are not mutually exclusive, thus each of the types on the left can be represented in examples from literature, but for the purposes of this chapter I have chosen to deal with each section separately, in order to suggest the course that the English and drama work might take. For those teachers who wish to emphasise pupils' own ideas and input it is possible to develop the theme without any reference to literature, perhaps taking the options under 'Reality' in the order they appear above, moving from the nucleus of the family to the world beyond, past, present and future:

CONFLICT: In the Family: Suggestions

Introductory Exercises
In pairs: Make friends - Argue - Make friends -
            Argue...
            Pupils choose, or are allocated identit-
            ies, as a stimulus for short scenes, eg:
            Grandparent - lodger; Babysitter - child;
            Mother in law - daughter in law; Grand-
            parent - grandchild.
(The danger here is obviously that of stereotyped interpretations, but these simple situations should help to ease pupils into the theme.)

'Openers'
'Has anyone seen my pipe/purse/tablets/keys...?'
'How much longer are you going to be in there?'
'How many times do I have to tell you...?'

Situations
The telephone call
The letter
Getting up/staying out late
Lending and borrowing
Asking favours
Rivalry/revenge
'The Confessional': priest/doctor/counsellor
The interloper
      It is particularly important that young and inexperienced pupils are asked to think seriously

about the nature of conflict within families. While
some of the more exuberant boys will be tempted to
move rapidly towards physical violence, they should
recognise that conflict is expressed far more commonly through the spoken word, through silence or
sulking or leaving the scene. Each of the situations can be developed in a number of ways. We
might, for example, introduce 'The interloper' by
asking pupils to suggest definitions of the word,
before comparing these with the dictionary's offering: 'Interloper...One who thrusts himself into any
position or affair, which others consider as per-
taining solely to themselves.' (Shorter Oxford English Dictionary) Pupils may then suggest inter-
lopers who or which immediately spring to mind from
books or the media: The prodigal son; Stig of the
dump; ET; the elderly relation in 'Crossroads'; the
lodger in 'Coronation Street'; the visitor from the
past (see, for example, Pinter's 'The Birthday
Party'); the alien disease or creatures of science
fiction; ghosts; the visitor in a time warp (see,
for example, Doctor Who); the stowaway; the child
(see, for example, Peter Nichols' 'A Day in the
Death of Joe Egg'). This work can obviously be
linked with Kafka's 'Metamorphosis' (see Chapter
Three). Pupils may choose any one of these types
and interpret it for themselves, or less obviously,
work with role cards where each member of the group
is assigned a role in the family, with one exception, to represent the interloper. The group may
develop an improvisation in which the family knows
in advance who the interloper will be and compare
this with the outcome when the intruder comes
unknown and unannounced.

CONFLICT: Neighbours

'Openers'
'Was that pigs I saw in your back garden?'
'I wonder if I could have a word about your Ernie?'
'I thought you ought to know that something strange
has come through from your cellar.'

Situations
Asking your next door neighbour for the first -
second - third time:

> Not to block your exit with his/her bike/car/
> ice cream van
> To stop his dog/cat/duck/rabbit destroying your
> plants

Not to throw snails/weeds/hedge clippings into
your garden
Not to train his/her telescope on your windows.

One of these situations may be followed through from
the first manifestation of the problem to the
climax, conceivably a court case. Pupils will inevitably have their own experiences to discuss and
develop and should also analyse the reasons why, as
a recent television documentary demonstrated, feuds
between neighbours are so common and so often get
out of hand. They should also consider the effects
of different kinds of housing: the tenement, high
rise flats, terraced street, detached estate and
commune.

CONFLICT: At Work

'Openers'
'Who's moved my test tubes/brief case/red box/mole
wrench...?'
'Who's in charge here, you or me?'
'That's not my job...I'm not paid to...'
'Shall we shop him?'

Registers
'Now Sir/Mrs Smith/son what seems to be the matter?'
'Yes m'lud/your honour/Jones/6329, that's correct
but...'
'Time ladies and gentleman, please.'
'Now come on Mrs Jenkins, eat up your porridge...'
'I'm sorry but I shall have to ask you to move Sir.'

Situations

Customer returns goods/clothes which have obviously
been used/worn
Customer and waitress/car salesman/hairdresser
Questioning the system
The picket line
Harrassment at work
Industrial sabotage

Each one of these ideas can be analysed and
elaborated, for example, we might introduce industrial sabotage by asking pupils to suggest jobs
which require that the workers co-operate as a team,
such as packing chocolate boxes on a conveyor belt,
cleaning the windows of a block of flats or planting
municipal flower beds. Pupils, working in groups,
then devise and demonstrate the sequence of actions

that constitute the task, at first silently, with
each member specialising in a particular process,
and then 'with the sound up', establishing names and
relationships. One worker is then nominated as the
saboteur. (Alternatively, role play cards may indicate this so that the odd man out will only be revealed in the course of the improvisation.) A signal
from the teacher or group can trigger the divergent
action which gradually throws the system into chaos,
or the saboteur may choose the moment for himself.
The third stage of the improvisation should explore
what happens next and how the workers attempt to
cope with their colleague's aberrant actions.

CONFLICT: In History

'Openers'
'You say this Anne of Cleves has the grace, the wit,
the beauty to be my Queen?'
'While you disport yourself, Sir Francis, the enemy
draws near.'
'You say this loathsome stew is tea? And at such a
price!'
'Bertie, this will not do. All London talks of your
frivolous pursuits.'

Situations
'What really happened':   Lady Godiva's ride through
                           Coventry
                           The disappearance of the
                           two little princes
                           The discovery of the Gun-
                           powder Plot
                           The start of the Great Fire
                           of London
     It helps of course if pupils are applying facts
that they have learned from their history lessons,
though some research will be necessary where the
topic is an unfamiliar one. Drama helps to take
history out of the sphere of the merely political
and chronological to present it in social, domestic
and personal terms and those events which are part
history, part legend, allow particular scope for
interpretation. Lady Godiva's ride is a good example.
     Any encyclopaedia will suggest enough of the
facts and the legend to provide a suitable basis for
drama work:

     Godiva (fl.1040-85), a lady who according to
     tradition rode naked through the streets of

> Coventry...Godiva, the wife of Earl Leofric,
> begged that he would lessen the burdomsome
> taxes on Coventry town. Leofric consented on
> condition that his wife would ride naked
> through the market when all the people were
> present. Godiva took him at his word and made
> the remarkable journey covered with nothing but
> her luxuriant hair. Her equally remarkable
> husband kept his promise and granted a remis-
> sion of the tolls...Some writers assert that
> Godiva ordered all to keep within doors during
> her ride, and that this was done; others that
> one man, the famous Peeping Tom, disobeyed and
> was very properly struck blind for his impert-
> inence; others again that a miracle made Godiva
> invisible! (Chambers Encyclopaedia)

Pupils should be able to identify the implicit dramatic confrontations here: Earl Leofric and Godiva's meeting; Godiva convincing her family and in-
laws of the importance of her ride; the unfortunate
groom fending off inquiries from local scandal-
mongers; the leading citizens meeting to try to decide how to keep the populace at bay and Earl Leofric's horrified realisation that Godiva is going
through with her threat. There are many more, for
the possibilities are legion; this is the stuff of
which pageants and musicals are made. Through such
dramatic explorations the characters, who may be
mere cyphers in history text books, acquire back-
grounds, foibles and feelings and inspire pupils to
undertake their own researches.

CONFLICT: In the Future

'Openers'
'Why he's born with blond hair. I thought I ordered
brown.'
'Sylvester, get up, you'll be late for videschool.'
'I really don't know what you see in that robot.'
'I'm sorry, only A category personnel are permitted
to view the intergalactic relay trials.'
'Where have you put my DTA?'

Situations

The twenty first century parliamentary debate
The last ticket to Mars
A broadcast debate: The ethics of cloning
Discrimination: Two hundred years on

Drama and the English Theme

Pupils might take the idea implicit in the
fourth 'Opener' and compare the class structure of
twentieth century Britain with the possible categor-
isation of the populace a hundred years from now
(with a sidelong glance at Huxley's 'Brave New
World' and Orwell's '1984'). This might involve an
analysis of the favoured characteristics then, and a
suggestion of these through advertising and propoganda, and a demonstration of what happens when an
inferior tries to challenge the system or a free
thinker contests the prevalent view of the history
of the twentieth century.

CONFLICT AND LITERATURE

The choice of possible literary stimuli is very wide
indeed since the resolution of conflict is the
thread which unites most plots. I have suggested
one possible, quite conservative, combination of
materials but the permutations are endless and, as
here, so many can be approached in different ways
with different age groups and ability levels. There
is only sufficient space to indicate some of the
ways a selection of these could be used to stimulate
English and drama work.

Noah's Ark
The pithy account of Noah's flood in Genesis is
stimulus enough for many and varied adaptations, as
later writers have demonstrated. One of the most
successful of these was the anonymous playwright
responsible for the six lively and whimsical pageants which form part of the Towneley cycle.[6] These
include his own version of the flood story, 'Processus Noe Cum Filiis', in which Noah is presented as a
comically vulnerable figure, bedevilled by a wife
who complains shrewishly and refuses to board the
ark until the flood waters threaten to drown her.
Pupils, like the Wakefield playwright, may choose to
see the story in human and comic terms, filling out
the narrative framework offered in Genesis and imagining how a fallible family might respond to such
cataclysmic events. They may take this one stage
further and choose to give the dramatisation an
overt moral apart from the obvious one of the reward
of virtue. Though much of the original Processus
Noe is difficult, pupils can appreciate something of
its vigour and vivacity with the help of an extract:

350   Noe: Full sharp ar thise showers
               That renys aboute.

<pre>
                        Therfor, wife, haue done; com
                        into ship fast.
          Uxor^a: _b Yei, Noe, go cloute thi shone!
                        The better will thai last.
  1 Mulier^c: Good moder, com in sone, for
                        all is ouercast,
                        Both the son and the mone.
  2 Mulier : And many wynd-blast
                        Full sharp.
                        Thise floodys so thay ryn;
                        Therfor, moder, com in.
      Uxor :   In fayth, yit will I spyn;
                        All in vayn ye carp.
</pre>

a = wife; b = Go mend your shoes!, ie Mind your own business!; c = daughter.

This should be read as expressively as possible in order to convey much of the meaning immediately. Pupils may then, in pairs or groups, attempt a paraphrase in clear, colloquial English. This could introduce an analysis, based on this and other Middle English samples, of the ways in which English has changed since the fifteenth century. The excerpt may decide the tone for the class's own dramatisations or may lead into a survey of the way other cultures have chronicled the great flood, notably the Assyrian, Sumerian, Babylonian and Greek versions. Less experienced groups may feel happier moving from written dramatisation or extension to drama work, while the more experienced may find the transition from improvisation to writing more stimulating. This last process resulted in a third year group collaborating to produce the script which has been appended. Pupils may also take a closer look at other possible arenas for conflict, not only that between Noah and his wife but between mother-in-law and daughter-in-law, father and son and predict the outcome when the whole of Noah's family, his wife's and daughters' families all attempt to climb aboard. They may debate, as Noah would have to, the definition of a 'living thing' and conjecture how Noah and his family might doubt and defend God's primitive reprisal as they witness their homes and friends sink beneath the waters. This introduces contemporary equivalents for the flood story, where a family appears to be singled out for especially arduous though preferential treatment by a superior force whose command must be obeyed.

'Beowulf'

'Beowulf' is an obvious contender for inclusion in

the theme: here the conflict extends beyond the verbal slanging matches of Processus Noe to the physical battles between Beowulf and Grendel and Grendel's mother. While teachers may happily encourage pupils to explore verbal manifestations of conflict, we tend to quail at the thought of pupils taking on monsters in the classroom. Of course there are confrontations, both explicit and implicit, in 'Beowulf' which do not require blows: the altercation between Unferth and Beowulf in King Hrothgar's hall and the professional jealousy between Beowulf's companions and Hrothgar's men, but the physical conflict can be approached safely if this is done in a suitably controlled way. The following paraphrase of Grendel's entry to Heorot offers excellent opportunities for mime:

Over the waste fens, the misty moorland, Grendel came stalking, that foul foe to men, that enemy of God. He put his giant hands to the great outer door; he thrust with power; the bars splintered like match-wood, the fire-hardened bolts burst assunder...Over the polished floor the monster prowled; a baleful fire burned in his eyes; grim joy shook him as he gazed upon the sleeping warriors. On a sudden he pounced; he caught up a sleeping man and tore him, limb from limb; there did he devour him whole; he drank the blood, he crunched the bones...[7]

Pupils, working in pairs, first identify and list the words which indicate the action, that is the verbs. This thus becomes a valid and painless exercise in identifying parts of speech. Once the verbs are identified, perhaps underlined, pupils can discuss and demonstrate the scope for action indicated by 'thrust', 'devour', 'drank' and 'crunched', and the difference between 'pounced' and 'caught', 'stalking' and 'prowled'. Pupils will need to decide how to convey the materials involved without representing them in concrete form. If the mime is successful the lack of real objects will not be felt. This exercise introduces the climax of the poem, Beowulf's victory over Grendel:

Then Grendel stretched a giant hand to where Beowulf lay; Beowulf seized it; in a mighty grasp he held it. Then for the first time the monster knew fear, never had he met such force in mortal man. He wrenched, he tugged; but

> Beowulf put forth all his might; grimly he held
> that evil one in his clutch...The foes grappled
> in deadly strife; this way and that they
> thrust, and swayed; against the walls they
> hurtled;...beside the benches they staggered..[8]

This combat can be ritualised, even choreographed,
with a narrator as accompaniment and performed so
that the combatants do not even need to touch. The
rest of the class can play the Danes, witnesses to
the fight. Another view of the scene can be presented through the eyes of these witnesses, describing
what they have seen, in retrospect, both immediately
after the event and in discussion with their grand-
children, many years later.

'Romeo and Juliet': Act III, Scene V

This is one of several scenes from this play alone
which might be chosen to display a facet of conflict. This scene can be extracted from the play
without too much damage to its meaning and Juliet's
opposition to her parents' choice of a husband reveals issues which are of universal interest. But
these are fairly superficial concerns; if the scene
had only these qualities to recommend it, Romeo and
Juliet would not be the remarkable play it is. The
scene should not be shoe-horned indiscriminately
into the theme; pupils should come away with some
understanding of the emotional power of the language
and recognise the ever increasing tension as Juliet
is forced deeper into deceit.
    The scene divides conveniently into sections:
Juliet's farewell to Romeo (1-64), Juliet's meeting
with her mother (65-125), Capulet's attack on his
daughter (126-203) and Juliet's plea for advice to
her Nurse (204-242). One possible approach to the
search for meaning in this scene, involves pupils
plotting the changing moods and tones, beginning
with the tender farewell of the lovers, at first
leisurely, but then hurried by the Nurse's entrance.
Pupils may note down the switches in tone and mood
opposite the line references and use this as a basis
for an improvised version of the scene which
attempts to reproduce the emotional climate through
a colloquial paraphrase. This may lead into an
informal test of pupils' understanding of the characters' motivation for acting as they do, where
pupils, in role, answer the audience's questions.
This should help to demonstrate that conflict within
a family is seldom polarised around right or wrong
answers but is fudged by misunderstanding, guilt,

social pressure and the best of intentions.

'A Poison Tree'
Despite the superficial simplicity of its structure,
Blake's poem is a difficult one since, as with so
many other 'Songs of Experience', the symbolism and
imagery are enigmatic and shifting. As meaning
begins to take shape it seems to slip again as the
metaphors accumulate:

> A Poison Tree
>
> I was angry with my friend:
> I told my wrath, my wrath did end.
> I was angry with my foe:
> I told it not, my wrath did grow.
>
> And I watered it in fears,
> Night and morning with my tears;
> And I sunned it with smiles,
> And with soft deceitful wiles.
>
> And it grew both day and night,
> Till it bore an apple bright.
> Any my foe beheld it shine,
> And he knew that it was mine,
>
> And into my garden stole
> When the night had veiled the pole:
> In the morning glad I see
> My foe outstretched beneath the tree.

Pupils can come closer to understanding such a poem
if they try to imagine it in pictorial terms; this
realisation becomes more potent if the poem is then
dramatised. There is no need to feed the pupils the
poem all at once; they can work on it verse by
verse, translating Blake's 'friend', 'wrath', 'foe'
and 'apple' into real entities. Where more than one
group chooses to work on the poem, it is worthwhile
displaying and contrasting the different interpretations the drama work will inevitably, and legitimately reveal. If some written record is thought
appropriate, pupils may describe and justify their
interpretation of the poem.
  The approaches described above represent only a
small selection from the many which could be used to
explore and compare different kinds of conflict.
They are all approaches which hold good for a wide
range of age groups and ability levels. There is no
reason why a whole class should necessarily concen-

trate on a single stimulus simultaneously; pupils, working in groups, might move in a cycle from one to another, or might choose to specialise in a particular area, sharing their work with the rest of the class. All the work described opens up opportunities for a wealth of written work and pupils should be given the chance to devise and decide written options for themselves. Since all the work involves planning, discussion and note-making, much of it can take place in the classroom; access to a hall or similar large space on one occasion a week would be sufficient to allow scope for all the activities described.

'Conflict' is a theme which is so broad that it can be seen as both literature based and 'reality' based. The two themes which are described in the remainder of this chapter have been chosen as examples which are more closely aligned to one pole or the other. 'Melodrama' has immediate and obvious links with a distinct literary genre; it would be difficult to explore the theme adequately without reference to literary conventions. 'The Street' can be seen as a more self-supporting theme, in the sense that literature here is more peripheral. It might be introduced to a first year class after reading Eve Garnett's 'The Family from One End Street', but it would be perfectly possible to broach the theme without a literary preamble. Here the emphasis is less on external literary relations and more on pupils' own imaginative input. We might say that 'Melodrama' is a response to an existing literary genre, while 'The Street' aims at developing pupils' own literature.

THE STREET

While this is a theme which might be used with almost any age group, this section will describe its possible development with a first year mixed ability class, since it seems to work particularly well in the lower school. It is assumed that pupils have little experience of drama and that the whole class is following the theme simultaneously. Access to the hall on one occasion a week will be needed for the 'lead' drama lesson which fires associated discussion and writing. The theme may commence in response to pupils' suggestions, to their class reader, to a particularly vivid piece of written work, as a follow up to a town survey, or exploration of housing through the ages, or in response to a controversial proposal to demolish a row of nineteenth century terraced houses. More obviously, it may begin, or indeed end, with a frieze depicting an imaginary street, produced in collaboration with the art department. Alternatively, pupils may find themselves in 'The Street' before they are aware that they are launching a theme which may account for several weeks English and drama work.

Week One: lead drama lesson

    A.   Walking in different ways: Pupils walk in different ways, meeting different people in an imaginary town.

    B.   Waiting

       a)   Alone at the bus stop: You are unsure if you are in the right place. A bus passes: you have been waiting at the wrong stop. Demonstrate your different moods in mime.

       b)   A cold morning: waiting for the bus to arrive. It is a long time coming and when it finally comes it is full and passes you by. (Mime)

       c)   As b) but now you are waiting with a stranger. Your shared frustration leads into a conversation as you wait for the next bus, which reveals that you live in the same street and have much in common.

       d)   The bus now arrives but there is room for one only. Politely justify why you, rather than your neighbour, should get on.

       e)   Repeat the process: this time politely justify why your neighbour should get on.

    C.   Pupils reveal what they have learned from c) and d) about where they live and who they are.

This information is used as a basis for the introduction of the theme. The class then describes and discusses the streets in which they actually live, the types of buildings, the amenities and the ways in which they meet their neighbours. The class moves on to describe their fictional street, which, for the time being, will be nameless. They are divided into six groups which will each specialise in a different area and produce as long a list as possible under their designated title:

         Housing: eg maisonette

Visitors: eg health visitor
Facilities: eg youth club
Hobbies: eg DIY
Problems: eg broken water main

In the next English lesson, these are read out and
neatly and attractively displayed in the classroom.
Each group then returns to its list and elaborates
this to describe the inhabitants, thus the health
visitor becomes a distinct individual, the youth
club leader acquires his own personal problems and
the maisonette is lived in by a couple with a past,
present and future. These elaborations are shared
with the rest of the class and form the raw material
for role play cards which will stimulate some of the
drama work which follows.

Week Two: lead drama lesson

A. Movement as, eg A business man, dustman
    carrying a heavy bin, postman, somnambul-
    ist, old person attempting to cross a busy
    street, a window cleaner.
B. Neighbours
    a) Pupils choose and mime an outdoor act-
        ivity which would be likely to bring
        neighbours into contact, eg cleaning
        the car, clipping the hedge, hanging
        out washing.
    b) In pairs, pupils each select one of the
        role play cards (face down) produced in
        the previous lesson. They discuss
        their role with their partners.
    c) While in the course of one of the act-
        ivities mimed in a), the two neighbours
        will fall into conversation, using and
        extending the information on the cards.
    d) Several pairs of pupils share what they
        now know of their identities with the
        rest of the class.
    e) Keeping their identities intact, the
        neighbours meet in a different context,
        eg off licence, doctor's waiting room,
        local shop.
    f) Keeping their identities intact and
        using similar contexts, pupils fall
        into conversation with a stranger who,
        they discover to their surprise, is a
        close neighbour.

This new information forms the basis for profiles of

the original pairs of neighbours, which are written up in the next English lesson. They form the nucleus for a network of family relationships which are presented diagrammatically and described in writing. Suddenly the inhabitants of the street are beginning to proliferate and the class decides that a complete and single record should be kept of their whereabouts. One pair of pupils therefore collaborates to compile the electoral roll and the pupil who has been playing the part of the local vicar begins to compile a record of births, marriages and deaths in the street. Finally, another pupil gleans from each inhabitant details of his or her home; this leads to the rough draft of a simple housing plan of the street, with occupants' names and professions listed beside each dwelling. Once the details have been finalised the final draft plan is displayed in the classroom.

Week Three: lead drama lesson

A. Pupils 'undress' in mime and get dressed: for school, as an athlete, police officer, mayor or mayoress, member of the armed forces, nurse etc and then move off in role.

B. Pupils return to their identities of Lead Lesson Two, which are now well developed. Working in groups of four or five, and having introduced themselves, the pupils choose an unusual situation which brings them together, for example, a heavy snow fall, a chimney fire, a road accident, a burglary. Pupils are asked to pay particular attention to the way they, in role, would be likely to react to such a situation and combination of personalities.

In the English lessons which follow, pupils are invited to describe, in retrospect, the unusual event depicted in their drama work, in the way in which their chosen character might, perhaps as a transcription of oral narrative, a letter, a diary entry, letter of praise or complaint to the local paper or local councillor, a witness's statement, a policeman's report, a journalist's article or a poem. Some pupils choose to script their improvisation, while others write first person accounts, in role, of their perceptions of their neighbours.

Week Four: lead drama lesson

A. Pupils mime the actions associated with a hobby or the work of their chosen character.

B. Some of the pupils have prepared large placards which mark the following areas in the hall: Doctor's waiting room, police station, post office, travel agency, local shop. Each pupil opts or is directed to one of these. Each group, so formed, will develop a scene which explores the inter-relationships of the personnel. Most pupils maintain their earlier identities, though some choose to play the staff involved. The scenes are staged, Medieval miracle play style, in their areas, the audience moving to each location in turn. When time permits, the audience is encouraged to question some of those involved.

In their English lessons, pupils produce a written record of the scene, choosing an appropriate form: the doctor's records, the travel agency forms or the appropriate part of the travel brochure, an account of what happened on holiday, the statement made at the police station, details of the missing animal or belonging, some of the personal advertisements placed in the shop window.

The theme could legitimately end here, with all the work incorporated into a classroom display and/or magazine, or, given sufficient class commitment, might be extended to consider other events in the life of the street: the election, the carnival, the street party, or the welcome extended to a famous ex-resident. Pupils might record a local 'Down Your Way' in which residents describe their community, work and interests and select an appropriate snatch of music. As with 'Conflict', the theme may be taken back or projected forward in time, to look at the nineteenth century antecedents or to imagine the twenty second century's equivalent of 'The Street'.

MELODRAMA

Although this is another example of a theme which could engross almost any age group, it is probably more suited to older pupils who can readily grasp the distinction between melodrama and tragedy and who can recognise pathos, hyperbole, bathos and sentimentality when they meet them. Some pupils may already understand the characteristics of the genre,

having taken part in a production, since melodramas
can make very successful school plays. Where this
is not the case, a look at extracts from representative nineteenth century melodramas will convey
something of the impassioned and inflated nature of
the language, the two dimensional nature of the
characters and the creaking coincidences of the
plots:

Mary   Mother, mother, where are you? Oh,
what do I see on the cold ground? It
can't be mother? Mother! (Approaches nearer) Mother! Oh, it can't
be my mother - she would hear me -
yet it looks like my mother. Oh
dear, it is. I know it can be no
other! Mother, mother! (Cries and
falls on her mother) Mother, why
don't you speak? Mother! (Kneels
and kisses her. Jane, recovering,
looks about her in wild disorder.)

Jane   Where am I?

Mary   Here, mother, on the cold ground!

Jane   (seeing her child) Ah, my child!
Bless you, bless you! But what are
we doing here in the open air?

Mary   You came out after father, mother.

Jane   Your father! (Screams) Ah, I now
remember all. They are tearing him
from me, to take him to a loathsome
dungeon! All now crosses me like a
wild dream. The factory - the red
sky - flames whirling in the air! My
eye-balls seem cracked - my brain
grows dizzy - I hear chains and
screams of death! My husband - they
shall not tear him from me!

('The Factory Lad, 1832)[9]

Henry   Villain! You are at present all-
powerful, I defenceless. But heaven,
who watches over all its creatures,
will never in the end suffer so
cowardly, heartless, and infamous a
man as yourself to triumph.

Hawkhurst Indeed! (To Ned Dawkins) Quick!
Open the trap, and descend with him
to the cellars. (At a sign from
Hawkhurst, several men rush upon
Henry. A desperate struggle. Henry
calls aloud for help. They gag his

mouth. The trapdoor is forced open, and Henry driven to the brink of the cellar beneath.)

Ned Hush! His cries have aroused the police.

Henry (Tearing off gag) The police! They come to my rescue. Help, help!
(They are forcing Henry down trap and forming a picture of consternation as act drop falls.)
('London by Night', 1868)[10]

Once students are aware that early serious silent films owed much to the melodramas of the nineteenth century, they should be able to suggest other elements themselves: the pure heroine threatened by the dastardly villain; the hero who is almost dull in his goodness; the ruthless father eager to sell his daughter into a life of misery and the mysterious stranger whose true identity is only revealed in the final scene. The list is a long one and these elements and others are delightfully parodied in Frank Muir's one acter 'The Grip of Iron'[11], which offers an excellent entré to the theme. This extract shows the hero, Sir Toby, revealing the truth about Lucy's wicked guardian, Silas Doom, a villain who specialises in carving the bones of his victims into chess men for sale:

Sir Toby Your guardian, my dear, is the man they know as "The Grip of Iron".
(Lucy totters and is about to faint. Sir Toby catches her and holds her to him.)

Sir Toby Don't worry, Lucy. I am here to protect you.

Lucy But my guardian - the strangler!

Sir Toby Yes and you are next on the list.

Lucy Me! But why me?

Sir Toby Because, Lucy, you are not just a little waif. You are heiress to a fortune. And he is after it!

Lucy So that's why he's kept me cooped up in the attic.

Sir Toby Yes. But don't worry. I am match enough for his villainies.

Lucy You, Sir Toby?

Sir Toby Yes. You see, I am not really Sir Toby Feltham, Baronet. My real name is...Honest Jack Strangeways, Bow Street Runner! (Sir Toby releases

139

> Lucy and bows to the audience. Then
> goes back and gets hold of Lucy
> again.)
> Sir Toby A law enforcement officer in the ser-
> vice of His Britannic Majesty, King
> George III.

'The Grip of Iron' displays in a condensed, accessible and amusing form, the techniques required of
the actors, the theatrical whisper, the repetition
of details ad nauseam so that nothing is misunder-
stood and a relish for dramatic irony and wonder-
fully unconvincing disguises. A close look at melodrama encourages pupils to identify the techniques a
playwright inevitably uses in order to develop the
plot and characterisation, and throws true tragedy
and more subtle writing into relief.

Once pupils have grasped the characteristics of
melodrama they are in a position to write, produce
and perform ones of their own, since melodrama lends
itself successfully to pastiche and parody, as 'The
Grip of Iron' demonstrates. While it is possible to
take the plot as a starting point, most students
find it easier to trace a narrative thread once the
characters are firmly in place. Some students will
enthusiastically launch into their own cast of characters, though most will require a little more
structured help. Since the range of possible char-
actors is disconcertingly wide, a tightening of the
net will help to focus a class's imagination. The
following short list is more than sufficient to inspire many possible plots: The hero, heroine,
villain, villain's wife, hero's mother, heroine's
parents, gipsy, ghost, and stranger. A melodrama
can feed off only three characters, as early silent
films have proved and where the cast is a larger
one, pupils can play more than one part. Melodramas
are best developed in groups, thus encouraging a
pooling of ideas. The students may begin with a
general discussion which results in a list of names
and series of role cards. Those who feel under-
confident may welcome half finished role cards,
which they are asked to complete:

Villain

Name: Age:

Residence:

His youthful antics drove his father to an

early grave. He cares for no one but himself and

Among his favourite past times are

He is ruthless but cowardly and particularly fears

He hopes to

This may be the appropriate time to introduce a model which suggests some of the possibilities, though on occasions, it is wiser to leave this until the students' first draft role cards are complete:

THE HERO: Justin Truelove

Age: 25

Handsome, gentle but brave when the occasion demands, and in love with Celestina Dawkins. His widowed mother, Ada, dotes on him. Celestina returns his love but their romance is doomed since her father knows he is poor. (Believes in honour, duty and his country!)

THE HEROINE: Celestina Dawkins

Age: 20

Beautiful only child, destined to inherit her father's ill-gotten wealth. She feels powerless to disobey her father's commands, but is in love with Justin. Their moonlight trysts have not been discovered - yet! Favourite colour: white.

THE VILLAIN: Sir Gerald 'Fetlocks'
              Jaggers

Age: 49

He has wantonly gambled away his inher-
itance and is irretrievably wicked and
dissipated. His wife has been driven
insane by his cruelty and is kept
hidden from the world. Desperate for
riches, he is determined to marry the
young, beautiful, innocent and RICH
Celestina. He is capable only of self-
love. Favourite colour: black.

THE VILLAIN'S WIFE: Amy Jaggers

Age: 31

Once as beautiful and pure as Celestina, her mind and beauty have been
destroyed by her husband's heartless
cruelty. She has a pitiful story to
tell, if only someone will listen,
but her incoherent ramblings win her
few friends. Only the doves, which
share her prison, see a softer, more
rational side to her.

THE HEROINE'S FATHER: Henry Leggitt
                      Dawkins

Age: 62

'Nouveau riche': tries hard to hide his
'vulgar' accent and doltish manners.
Longed for a son, but has had to make
do with Celestina, whom he sees as a
marketable commodity. His wife is
unaware of his disreputable friends
and of his infidelity with 'Lusty Lou',
the barmaid at the 'Egg and Maypole'.

THE HEROINE'S MOTHER: Florence Dawkins

Age: 55

Plain, inarticulate, but before her
marriage vivacious and gregarious. She
was tricked into marriage and fears her
husband, who has totally cowed her.
She is bemused by her daughter's charm
and beauty and wonders where it can
have come from.

THE HERO'S MOTHER: Ada Truelove (née
                   Spritts)

Age: 57

Ada gave birth to twelve children but
three died in infancy, two were wrongly
imprisoned for theft, three have left
to find their fortunes elsewhere, one
is feared lost in an avalanche, and two
have broken their mother's heart, which
leaves Justin and explains Ada's devo-
tion to him.

THE GIPSY: La Donna Esmeralda

Age: difficult to tell under all that
     make-up

She comes offering tales of the future
and leaves disclosing news of the past.
Hers are no ordinary gifts and her
companion is no ordinary astrologer.
She is a consummate liar but will do
everything in her power for those she
likes.

THE STRANGER: Identity to be revealed

Age: ?

He arrived when his help was most
needed and offered it without hope of
recompense. His tattered appearance
seems to belie a certain nobility of
bearing and his obvious intelligence
suggests better times and lost opportunities. His interest in the whereabouts of the villain's wife indicates
a man with a mission.

THE GHOST

Age: Ghosts don't count the years

This is no ordinary ghost: for a start
he has a sense of humour and a thick
skin. He tends to appear at precisely
the wrong moment to quite the wrong
person. He has his own very personal
problems, but with all the fuss about
Justin and Celestina, who is going to
listen to a neurotic ghost?

Once the cast list is complete, students may choose
to specialise in a particular role, filling out the
bare bones of the role cards and jotting down
further details, in rough, after checking them with
other members of the group. Each student can then
prepare a short speech which introduces the character to the audience, whether the small group of
players or the remainder of the class. Initially,
the emphasis will be on polishing the content,
producing a vivid portrait of the character, but
then attention should turn to delivery, since each
character will require his own voice, and this
should be exaggerated. It will help if students
have already read, and perhaps recorded, a melodrama. The short speeches will demand stylised
gestures, the hand on heart of the heroine, the
villain who brandishes his stick or the clenched
fist of the heroine's father. The speeches can

develop into an effective performance in themselves; they are best delivered from a conventional
stage, where each character can emerge from the
wings or from behind the curtain, sporting a few
simple articles of costume, the villain's black
cape, the heroine's white veil or the gipsy's ear-
rings. The audience will play its part too, for
melodrama offers excellent opportunities for audience participation and comment. They should be
prepared to listen attentively but may be permitted
to boo and hiss appropriately and to offer consola-
tion and advice to the victims. Music will add a
new dimension, whether composed and performed by the
students to fit the mood of the moment, or extracted
from commercial recordings.[12]

By this stage, the plot possibilities should be
apparent to each of the groups, and even a single
role card may be sufficient to demonstrate the
course of the main plot. This student's description
of the heroine is an obvious example:

Desdemona Cinderberry

Age: 19

Eldest daughter of the eight children of
Gladys and William Cinderberry. Not happy
at home: she is like Cinderella and has to
do the housework and look after her brothers
and sisters, while her mother gives tea
parties. She earns money sewing clothes
but her father spends it on the race course.
She loves the hero, Captain John Isgood, and
is waiting for the chance to make her escape.

A description of a minor character may suggest a
sub-plot:

The Stranger

An Indian gentleman with an air of power and
mystery. Talks very little and reveals even
less. He is really the Maharaja of Ranjipur
and he has vowed to follow the hero to pay him
the debt he owes him, because Captain Isgood
saved his family and his people from disaster.

Just as the characters are built up gradually, so
there are several stages between the initial idea
for a plot and the dramatisation and conceivably,
script. The plot may be built around a model or

parallel, for example fairy tales like Cinderella or The Little Match Girl, or may develop from an idea for a first, middle, or final scene. Where students have used the role types suggested, and need some stimulus for dramatisation, a possible plot outline may help:

'Melodrama'

Characters: Hero - Heroine - Villain - Hero's Mother - Heroine's Mother, Father - Villain's Wife - Ghost - Gipsy - Stranger.
    Optional extras: Lusty Lou - Astrologer - Tramp - Inn-keeper - and any suggestions of your own.
    You may take on more than one part, where this is feasible.

Scene One: Heroine Heroine's Mother Heroine's Father Location? (Throughout, characters are either on stage or are talked about. Extra char- acters can, of course, be added.)	This scene should make clear the rela- tionship between the characters, and the parents' attitude to their daugh- ter and any prospective marriage. Possible questions for consideration: Do the parents know of the heroine's love for the hero? How will the hero- ine convey her feelings and plans to the audience without disclosing all to her parents? How will the heroine escape to meet the hero in the next scene?

Scene Two: Hero Heroine Ghost Location?	Hero and heroine should display their undying love for each other, the pathos of their predicament and their plans for the future. Try to contrast their attitudes, eg who is the more realistic/pessimistic/ altruistic, etc? What part does the ghost play? Does he modify their ideas and actions?

Scene Three: Villain	This should reveal the relationship between the villain and his wife and

146

Villain's wife Gipsy Stranger Location?	his plans, as expressed to her, and as disclosed, more candidly, to the audience. What part do the gipsy and the stranger play? Do they appear on stage simultaneously? Do they affect the villain's ideas and actions?
Scene Four: Hero Heroine Villain 'Witness', eg Gipsy/ Ghost/ Stranger, etc.	'The Complication': The villain will now do something which challenges the hero's courage and endangers the heroine. What is this challenge? What are the constraints which make it difficult for the hero to circumvent the villain's schemes? What will the witness do with the information gathered?
Scene Five: Heroine Villain Heroine's Father (and poss- ibly Mother)	The heroine is endangered by the villain's fiendish schemes. How is her father/mother involved? How will the villain's pride and arrogance eventually help to bring about his downfall?
Scene Six: Hero Hero's Mother Ghost/Gipsy/ Stranger	The hero at his lowest ebb. He would have capitulated completely if not for...? Hero resolves to fight back (not necessarily physically). His plans revealed to the audience: he hopes to rely on the power of good, the villain's self-destructive pride and a smidgen of common sense. Much dramatic irony is helpful here, eg we know the hero's plans may come to naught because of the villain's superior cunning.

Scene Seven:
Hero
Heroine
Villain
Heroine's
  Mother
Hero's
  Mother
	'The Confrontation' and climax: The hero and heroine nearly meet a grisly end but miraculously escape with the help of the hero's tenacity, good luck etc, though even the hero's and heroine's mothers have a fortuitous part to play in bringing about the happy ending. Any suitable character

Drama and the English Theme

'The Witness'	may act as 'Witness': his/her comments will heighten the tension and suspense and the audience's involvement in the scene.
Scene Eight: All the char- acters may appear on stage, how- briefly, during the penultimate scene	'Resolution and Reconciliation': The villain is suitably punished. The most unhappy and virtuous find unex- pected happiness. Much is revealed of the past and misconceptions are aired and dispelled. Comic relief helps to lighten some of the tension.
Scene Nine: Hero Heroine (and perhaps Ghost, lurk- ing)	'Conclusion and Commentary': Both characters provide a coda to the pre- ceding events and look at their own futures and the nature of good and evil. They should leave the audience with a self-satisfied feeling that right has triumphed and poetic and moral justice still exist - if only in melodramas.

The plot outline may be presented absolutely complete, or as here, key facts may be omitted, so that
students can finalise these for themselves. The
more experienced, or the more inspired the group,
the more we can afford to omit. Such a plot outline
can be presented as an informal prediction exercise
where each group is given it in sections, scene by
scene, and is asked to foresee the possibilities for
development. It helps enormously if students are
given a visual model for their work, ideally a video
recording or an early silent film which runs through
the stages outlined above, from exposition, through
complication, to crisis and confrontation and eventual resolution. Improvising and scripting a complete melodrama is a demanding and time-consuming
enterprise, and if the goal is understanding the
genre and the pleasure derived from group composi-
tion and dramatisation, rather than a complete and
polished performance, then the working out of a
single representative scene may be sufficient
reward.

Just because melodrama does not require subtle
acting skills, because it legitimises ham gestures

and the unconvincing plot, students seem to find it a reassuring dramatic form. While it allows ample scope for the extrovert's talents, it also contains niches for those who are naturally retiring. Ideally though, pupils should not be type cast and melodrama works best as a theme when the introverted are sufficiently inspired to step outside their inhibitions and surprise their peers, and themselves, with their skills in ranting and wailing, 'wreeling and writhing'.

NOTES

1.   Ann and James Owen, Mainspring English 1 and 2 (Evans, 1982).
2.   Peter Knott, Outlook: Themes for Writing (John Murray, 1982).
3.   See, particularly, The English Project (Ward Lock Educational).
4.   See, for example, 'Myself', described in Chapter 10 of this author's Teaching English (Croom Helm, 1982).
5.   Betty Jane Wagner, Drama as a Learning Medium (Hutchinson, 1979).
6.   A.C. Cawley (ed.), The Wakefield Pageants in the Towneley Cycle (Manchester University Press, 1958).
7.   Retold by Leila Davies in Living Language (BBC Radio for Schools, 1972).
8.   Ibid.
9.   John Walker, 'The Factory Lad: A Domestic Drama in Two Acts' (1832) in James L. Smith (ed.), Victorian Melodramas (Dent, 1976).
10. Attributed to Charles Selby, 'London by Night: A Drama in Two Acts', reprinted in James L. Smith (ed.), Victorian Melodramas (Dent, 1976).
11. Found in Frank Muir and Simon Brett, Frank Muir Goes Into Christmas (Star Books, 1979).
12. See, for example, Sounds Effects Number 22: Music for Silent Movies, Dennis Wilson; Sounds Effects Number 16: Disaster. Both BBC Cassettes (BBC Enterprises).

Chapter Seven

THE MASS MEDIA AND COMMUNICATIONS STUDIES

THE MASS MEDIA

Teachers of English are only too aware of the importance and influence of the mass media. They are
tired of being told that their pupils spend as much
time in front of a television as they do in the
classroom and weary of depressing statistics which
seem to hint at their responsibility for somehow
inoculating children against the creeping media
disease. It is the foolish and unusual teacher of
English who condemns the media as fiercely and
famously as Denys Thompson and F.R. Levis once did[1].
We are more likely to agree with Richard Hoggart
that it makes little sense to distinguish between
high culture and popular culture, and to set the
school's values against those of the mass media.
Rather, the discrimination should take place within
the media, between the 'processed' and the 'living',
the 'authentic' and the 'phoney'[2]. No teacher of
English can afford to deny an interest in the mass
media, nor neglect to encourage a discriminating
response to its products, products which, like English, testify to the all-importance of the spoken
and written word. Michael Marland is right in
suggesting that,

> no middle school English course would be com-
> plete today without the integration of the
> newer media into the classroom consideration.
> Last night's television play and today's news-
> paper must take their place in a continuum that
> ranges from the most trivial of reading matter
> to the most major literature.[3]

Gone, we assume, are the days when, according to
Hilde Himmelweit's findings, only six per cent of

150

teachers ever talked about television in the class-room[4]. But while teachers of English can and do manage the integration which Michael Marland describes, we find it harder to introduce the alto-gether more ambitious media based teaching which the authors of the Schools Council Mass Media Project advocate:

> In our view, media based teaching should aim to do three things, firstly, to encourage pupils to be discriminating in their role as consum-ers; secondly to give them some insight into the development and workings of the contempor-ary mass media; and thirdly, wherever possible, to give pupils the opportunity to originate and produce their own mass media materials.[5]

It is not difficult to see why teachers of Eng-lish and others have failed to introduce curriculum initiatives on these lines. The school and the Eng-lish curriculum are already so congested that only priorities can survive and we are all subject to society's, parents', pupils', examiners' and employ-ers' expectations of what we should, and signific-antly should not, be teaching. Where 'with drama there was a tradition going back fifty years or more for the outstanding English department to make some form of drama a keystone of its work'[6], media studies are seen as upstarts, lacking academic and vocational credibility. A study of the mass media can leave many English teachers feeling insecure. We may feel that our degree courses have equipped us to teach Shakespeare or Lawrence but they seldom develop the analytical tools required for a study of the media. We will agree with the Newsom Report that 'it would be wrong to leave pupils with the idea that everything they like is bad, or that all criticism is negative'[7] but we will also be wary of going to the other extreme of appearing to toady to our pupils' tastes in order to win superficial approval. It is the misguided teacher who pretends a knowledge of teenage magazines or who patronises pupils by playing a pop record as an easy stimulus for creative writing.

The main obstacle in the path of the fully fledged media studies course is a practical one,

> The main difficulty facing schools is lack of resources...There are still many schools which do not even have an adequate supply of books, let alone such equipment as portable tape

151

recorders, film cameras and video-tape facilities. Without a substantial increase in funds
many of the more adventurous media-based creative work called for here cannot be put into
practice.[8]

Len Masterman's excellent 'Teaching about Television'[9] is persuasive and comprehensive and many
teachers of English would love to attempt the course
he suggests, but the equipment required is daunting.
How far away we are from equipping ourselves prop-
erly for media studies is suggested in a recent
NATE survey[10] which reports that tape recorders and
video machines are either defective or unavailable
in many schools and finds that many English teachers
have to stagger with books and equipment from class
to class. Given these deficiencies it is little
wonder that many teachers of English confine 'media
studies' to reviews of television programmes and the
class newspaper. This is a start, since it at least
recognises the significance of these products in our
pupils' lives; the danger is that we will allow a
dearth of equipment to inhibit any attempt to bring
consideration of the media into the classroom.
    The lack of videorecorders, videocameras and
television studios should not prevent pupils understanding how, for example, the different broadcasting authorities work, or analysing the editorial
policies of different newspapers and radio channels
and learning about the psychological bases for much
advertising. And there are course books which help
to make this possible.[11] More fundamentally though,
pupils will be in a better position to discriminate,
appreciate and understand the mass media if they are
encouraged to create for themselves. Just as the
Newbolt Report[12] sensibly pointed out that, 'A class
that has composed and acted its own plays is in a
much better position to read other plays', so the
pupil who has faced the editorial decisions which
commonly confront the news editor should be able to
recognise the bias inherent in any medium which must
select for publication or broadcast from a mass of
possible material. Drama has close natural links
with the mass media, notably with radio and television. It allows opportunities for the creation,
selection and presentation of materials and for the
types of decision making that are involved in broadcasting. The exercises which are described in the
sections which follow are examples of the kind of
drama work which can be attempted where equipment
and even space are minimal. Alternatively, they can

be seen as introductory exercises for extended and more ambitious media courses.

Television, English and Drama

Television is the most pervasive and influential of the mass media; it is the source for many of our pupils' ideas and the form in which most pupils meet most fiction. While it has undoubtedly distracted many pupils from reading at home, television has also spurred pupils to read books associated with popular programmes. The 'Grange Hill' and 'Tucker' books are obvious examples of this, and it is significant that it takes a successful television adaptation to repopularise a literary classic. Indeed, 'it seems impossible for English teachers to deny their interest in language in the media, or to refrain from a cultural critique of those products of the media in which language plays the dominant role.'[13] Television's importance should be acknowledged whenever we are contemplating language, fiction or drama in the classroom. The 'cultural critique' of television's products may be modest, for example, James Bracey, Head of English at Wandsworth School, uses television as an ally in promoting reading and encouraging discrimination:

> Knowing that many of his children come from households where there are no books, he works on the material that is available to them at home - newspapers and television. 'Each week they write criticisms of a programme they've seen and read them out in class. Then I read them reviews of the same programme from, say, the Sun and the Guardian, wanting them to recognise the difference and hoping that next time they will pick up the paper and read the review for themselves'.[14]

While pupils may not share the same reading interests, they will have in common a small number of popular television programmes, and teachers of English and drama have always known that if they wish to make a point about plot construction or characterisation, reference is best made to these programmes if all the class is to understand what is being described.

One of our aims must be to help pupils to understand something of the way television works and to present their views about television programmes in a reasoned and articulate manner. We must first analyse what pupils know or think they know about television and decide what we wish them to know. This might be broached by pooling all the class's immediate knowledge and identifying those areas where there is disagreement or ignorance. This might begin with an informal quiz which focusses on such matters as the dates when different channels came on air, the meaning and role of the IBA, ITV, BBC, ITN and the differences between networked and non networked programmes. This may develop into a more open-ended discussion concerning the differences between the four channels, which allows pupils to air glib generalisations, before turning to a more careful survey of the programmes which are actually on offer in any week, with the help of the Radio and TV Times. Pupils, working in pairs or groups, will need to devise their own sub-headings for different categories of programmes and will then decide the proportion of each offered on each of the four channels. They are then in a better position to look at their own attitudes to television: how much television they actually watch, the influence television has had on how they spend their leisure hours, the contribution television has made in feeding them significant ideas. This may develop into an inquiry into more fundamental issues, for example, into the difference between fact and fiction on television. Pure fiction is usually easy to identify, but 'fact' should cause pupils more problems as they attempt to categorise a day's or week's programmes.

Pupils can make their own lists of what they consider to be the most commonly voiced criticisms of television, for example:

There is too much sport on television
There are too many repeats
There are too many imported American programmes
There are too many 'clashes' between channels
Television paints a distorted picture of contemporary society

While 'too many' and 'too much' are inevitably value laden and subjective, 'Too much in relation to what?' we might ask, pupils can still suggest whether or not they consider these criticisms to be fair and can assess whether something can be done to appease those complaining or whether these complaints are inevitable, given only four channels and stringent financial restrictions. Pupils will need to anticipate whether the coming of cable television and satellite broadcasting will affect these phen-

omena. They can try to unravel the implicit messages of television by taking a belief which they
hold or which is prevalent, for example, that those
who speak Oxford English are more intelligent than
those who speak with a regional accent, that the
north is somehow not as civilised or 'with it' as
the south, and trying to decide, and it can be no
more than an attempt, the source for this impression, whether family, friends, experience, television, radio, films, books, magazines, the press or
advertising. This may lead into an attempt to
decode television's signals and images; it obviously
helps here if pupils can view together a magazine
programme, although a certain amount can be achieved
from memory alone. The class may first take an
overall view of a night's viewing and then concentrate on one programme; this work could obviously be
done as homework. Some of the more common observa-
tions to emerge might be:

> Gardening experts are allowed, even expected,
> to have regional accents. Newsreaders, includ-
> ing those in regional magazine programmes,
> seldom do.
> Breakfast television assumes that its viewers
> want an informal, less intellectually strenuous
> kind of programme.
> Women experts on sport are merely tolerated by
> their male colleagues.
> 'Normal' life makes for boring television and
> there is no such thing as true 'fly on the
> wall' television.

Pupils may choose to move from here to concentrate
on a single programme or type of programme, breakfast television, the party political broadcast, the
children's magazine programme or quiz shows, in
order to assess what these programmes have in common
and how they differ, both within and between types.
This will involve analysing techniques, presentation, gimmicks, personnel and sequencing. Pupils
may look particularly closely at the registers of
each, recreating these themselves on tape. They
will know that the style adopted by the compère in
'Family Fortunes' would be quite inappropriate for
the newsreader in 'Newsnight', but they should also
be able to describe the differences in style which
distinguish 'Quote Unquote' (Radio Four) from 'Play
Your Cards Right' (ITV One) and 'Call My Bluff' (BBC
Two). Pupils should also be aware of the way in
which the type and tone of programme is related to

when it is broadcast, early morning, early after-
noon, early evening or late at night.

Before moving on to look at the philosophy
behind the sequencing of television programmes in
any evening, pupils should have the opportunity to
try their hands at this themselves, bearing in mind
the built in constraints and external competition.
They can take any week day at random and compare BBC
and ITV schedules, discussing these in groups and
making explicit the philosophy, the rationale which
appears to underlie each, from the simplest: people
want to hear the news soon after they come in from
work, to the more sophisticated notion of the nine
o'clock watershed after which sex and violence are
more acceptable, and the fact that one channel will
attempt to 'hook' viewers early in the evening.
This could logically lead into a role play exercise
where the 'Viewers' and Listeners' Association'
confronts the controller of one of the channels with
their complaints and comments, based on a week's
sample viewing, where the director is required to
defend the corporations' decisions. This can be
prefaced by a reconstruction of the meetings in
which both sides marshal their arguments, prior to
the confrontation. Alternatively, the group may
stage the meeting when a freelance director of a
controversial television programme attempts to convince a directorial panel that it is worthy of
broadcast on their channel.

Those pupils who have realised their own ideas
or scripts via drama are in a better position to
appreciate critically the professional offerings of
television and radio. Those pupils who have an
understanding of the roles and potential for influence of the writer, screenplay writer, director,
designer, actor and editor should have a clearer
understanding of the scope and constraints which
face producers and directors in radio and television. Pupils should be able to discern how light-
ing and editing, for example, may make or mar the
interpretation of a script or concept. They should
grasp the surprising amount of freedom that even the
most precise of writers leaves to the interpreter,
both the director and actors and the viewer or
listener at home. Pupils can begin to explore this
through simple simulations. In the first, a one act
play, ideally a pupil's own, which is intended for
television dramatisation, is discussed at an
informal meeting involving the producer/director,
designer, leading actors and playwright. All have
had time to read the play and to note down their

immediate impressions, which will help to decide the finished gloss given to the text. All the pupils involved in the simulation will already have a good idea of the role of each of their colleagues and will understand the constraints which they face: censorship, questions of taste, economics, and the time and space available. The decisions are documented and one of the scenes is tried out to see whether these decisions have to be rescinded in the light of what actually transpired 'in rehearsal'.

In the second simulation the group starts with an idea which comes from the director. This may be a very simple one, for example, 'A Day Trip on a Ferry to Boulogne'. Each group of pupils is fed this idea but with a distinct angle:

> One of a series of 'documentary' programmes designed for BBC 2 and entitled 'Days Out'.
> A satirical play which ridicules the mores of sections of the British populace.
> A pilot programme for a comedy series for ITV in which the leading characters will reappear over a number of weeks.
> An introductory programme for a soap opera which will deal with the tensions and conflicts on board a cross Channel ferry.

The simulation focusses on the planning meeting when the story line and characters are negotiated; this may lead immediately into the improvisation of a key scene.

Of course, pupils will never completely understand the television director's, camera man's or editor's role unless they are involved in making their own television programme. For those, many, English teachers who count themselves lucky if they can wheedle away the video-taperecorder twice a term, this will be impossible, but pupils can be encouraged to consider seriously the importance of editing in deciding the nature of the message broadcast through some single exercises: Pupils can begin by adopting the procedure used by most intelligent job applicants, and particularly those facing a demanding interview. This involves identifying the applicant's plus and minus points; these can be listed, with a particular job in mind, and used as a basis for a letter of application which boosts the plus points and deliberately omits or 'edits' the minus points. Pupils can move from these angled views of themselves to similar views of their school, town or village. In the first, one of these is presented favourably as it might be to attract parents, tourists or industrialists. Images are carefully selected and where filming or photographing these is made impossible, pupils can describe and sketch the image with suitable captions underneath. In order to explore the point that where any complex entity is concerned, many viewpoints are possible, pupils can present a hostile view, perhaps from the angle of someone opposed to comprehensive schools or attacking the insular and provincial nature of a small market town. The hostile view of the village might suggest that the pastoral idyll of the sleepy hamlet is far from the truth, or is anathema to anyone in search of a vigorous and stimulating community. The picture of the school can begin as a generalised one, taking an overall perspective, before moving on to concentrate on certain sections, perhaps the assembly, the dinner queue, gym lesson or day trip out. Groups of pupils can discuss the television techniques they would use to convey a particular message, for example, close up shots of key personnel at important moments, cutting from one activity to another, omitting significant incidents, using voice over to train the viewer's response. This can lead into an investigation of the influence of the narrator or voice over in distorting and reinforcing what is seen. Pupils can try this for themselves by producing a sequence of speech and action, for example, an incident at a police station, in the dinner queue or outside a court. This is then performed to the rest of the class with the 'volume' turned down but with a narrator dubbing a specific, biassed interpretation of events. The enaction is repeated accompanied by a different narration. Finally, the group performs the original scene as intended and without a narrator so that the three versions can be compared and discussed. The voices, tones and even stances of the narrators can be varied in order to decide their importance and influence; the narrator may appear as a John Pilger figure, stamping his reputation and identity on the scene or, at the other extreme, may be an anonymous and disembodied voice.

Pupils can contrast this kind of editing with the kind used in newspapers, where ideological bias, the space and time available, the quality of the data and the journalist's skills will decide what is reported and what omitted. The class may begin with their own incident or with a newspaper account; local papers provide the best examples. Each group can devise one witness's version of the truth and dramatise that, imagining that the witness is the major source for the journalist's story and showing the effect this angle has on the reporting of events by producing the finished newspaper copy. This is then compared with another version of the 'truth', suggested by another likely witness, which is again presented and recorded as if in the newspaper.

Advertising

It has become commonplace for teachers introducing 'Advertising' into the classroom, to appear clutching a large collection of newspapers, magazines and colour supplements and to proceed to ask the class to identify the techniques of persuasion employed by advertisers to induce consumers to buy the products and services. This usually involves pupils ticking off examples of appeals to snobbery, intelligence, status, sex appeal, group cohesion, fear and so forth. By the time they arrive at the fourth year pupils may have gone through this process, in a rather perfunctory and desultory manner, many times over, wondering quite what the point of it all is. The exercise often leaves pupils vaguely bewildered since they are not sure whether or not they are supposed to resist all advertisements, since the techniques are apparently so devious. An isolated 'technique spotting' exercise is useless since advertising is not put into any sort of economic framework. It does not, for example, demonstrate why advertising is so necessary in underpinning all industry, including broadcasting and the press; it does not attempt to investigate whether advertising is an arbiter, initiator, or merely a reflector of cultural patterns and social values.

It helps enormously if pupils can visit an advertising agency or at least talk to an advertising copy writer, but, failing this, they should be provided with information concerning the development of a television or commercial radio advertisement through its gestation to the final broadcast product. Pupils can demonstrate their understanding of this by winding the process back and simulating the production themselves, taking on the roles of the personnel involved and demonstrating how key decisions were reached. Rather than looking at advertising exclusively from the consumer's point of view, as so often in the classroom, pupils can thus begin to look at the process from the inside out. The need for caution when interpreting advertisements comes across much more emphatically where pupils are aware of the assumptions, processes and decision-making involved in producing advertisements, and particularly those destined for television and radio.

Pupils can try their hands at making their own advertisements, dramatising the process from the initial idea, presented at a group meeting, to the finished product, ideally filmed, but where this is impossible, presented to an audience or recorded as if for commercial radio. Pupils will need to be aware of the advantages and limitations of their prospective medium, whether radio or television, and will have to devise ways of minimising the disadvantages. For example, both media are ephemeral and the message will need to be reinforced if it is to have impact. Colour will have to be conveyed through sound, over the radio, and pupils will need to avoid clichéd and debased techniques and falling foul of the IBA's advertising code. Where pupils choose to introduce a new product, they will need to define its uniqueness in relation to existing competitors. They may choose to sell an existing product in a novel way, perhaps bringing status appeal into the advertising of a bath cleaner, or may look at the precedents for selling famous products, including Pears soap, Guinness and Heinz beans, before inventing a novel angle for promoting these in the late 1980s.

A historical enquiry may take pupils back to the introduction of staple products such as tea and tobacco; they can imagine and dramatise the spread of their fame and prestige. Pupils may attempt the apparently impossible, promoting nonsensical products and creating new crazes, as happened in the USA in the 1960s, when the notion of buying bottled air and 'pet rocks' was hyped. The assignment may be structured by feeding pupils a particular angle: 'Your advertising technique must intrigue your audience but not bewilder them to the point of frustration'; 'Introduce an element of surprise at some point...'; 'Invert the techniques of your competitors - pretend you do not need to stoop to their devices'; 'Shock your viewers in the interests of health and safety'. Pupils may demonstrate how a single product or service can be advertised in many ways, where each dramatisation of the advertisement uses a different appeal, fear, envy, snobbery, quality, economy or validation by the famous. The distortion which is inevitable whenever advertisement is involved and time is short, can be demonstrated when the audience, the potential consumers, are encouraged to question the producers of the product and the advertisement.

Any study of advertising should expose the norms and ideals projected by television advertisements, in particular, for these are more influential and potentially more dangerous than the hyperbole employed to sell a particular product. Obvious examples are, the notion of the normal family, which is quite at odds with the complex nature of contemporary family life; the role of women in advertisements, and the reinforcement of WASP attitudes. Drama can make explicit the narrowness of these projections, where pupils show the 'advertisers'' family at breakfast, on a picnic or responding to a new product before contrasting this with a more likely and normal response.

In the past there has been a tendency to assume that the teacher has already been inoculated by maturity, intelligence and training against advertisements, that we are impervious to their blandishments and that, since our pupils are still vulnerable to infection, a quick course in their English lessons is the booster jab they need. The truth, of course, is far more complex since none of us is immune and we all buy products, use services, in response to advertisements. Not all advertisements are gross distortions, nor are all advertisers villains and our pupils are far more sophisticated consumers than many of us would like to concede. An investigation into advertising should not consist of the imposition of the teacher's opinions and an interminable list of jaundiced caveats, rather it should be an exploration and a crystallisation of the individual's perceptions and assumptions through a sharing of these with others, through **drama.**

Television News Reporting

As teachers of English, we tend to treat advertising as the great ogre and perpetrator of untruths, to the virtual exclusion of news reporting, when, as Len Masterman and others have suggested,

> nowhere does that great illusion of television as a presenter of unmediated reality have greater general credibility than in news presentations. Nor in any other field of television is the illusion quite so sedulously fostered by the broadcasting organisations. In no other area of television education therefore is it quite so incumbent upon the teacher to demonstrate to his students the constructed nature of what they see.[15]

It is not until pupils attempt to present 'news' to
their colleagues that they begin to realise the
extent to which selection, interpretation, and
therefore bias, must be involved. Few of us will
have access to the sorts of facilities used in the
recent University of Nottingham news project, which
involved local school children presenting the news
using closed circuit television, but that is no
reason for neglecting the issue altogether. Where
commercial news simulation packs exist, they tend to
be beyond the means of all but the most fortunate of
English teachers, but pupils can help to build their
own simulations with some help from the teacher.
This presupposes that we know what the exercise
intends to demonstrate:

1. That the concept 'news' is a difficult one
   to tie down; it is shifting and unspecific.
   When we talk of news we have in mind what
   is fed to us through the news channels and
   we have no way of measuring how objectively
   news-worthy this is. What emerges as news
   is the product of a complex series of perceptions, including what the news editor
   and colleagues see as news and what their
   rival news gatherers and producers define
   as news. Just asking pupils to discuss and
   define 'news' should be a salutory exercise
   in itself.
2. That whatever is presented as the news represents only a tiny and subjectively selected proportion of the events which reach
   the news-gathering agencies, and, as soon
   as a selection is made, bias and distortion
   inevitably creep in.
3. That every reporter, every middleman, who
   comes in contact with the news immediately
   changes it in some way. As soon as the
   news is reported and recorded it is medi-
   ated into something else and invested with
   the patina of received wisdom by news-
   casters whom we are encouraged to trust.
4. That there is a pecking order in the way
   the news is ordered. More 'significant',
   cataclysmic events come first; domestic
   disasters take precedence over foreign disasters of a similar magnitude; once an
   important story has been reported it will
   tend to be followed up to its conclusion;
   quirky, whimsical and good news will tend
   to come near the end of the broadcast, with

the sports reports and before any weather report. Implicit in this is the notion that news, by and large, is equated with ill tidings.

5. That we have certain preconceptions and assumptions about the way the news should be reported. It should be delivered in a suitably formal, dignified and ostensibly 'objective' manner; the newscaster's opinions should not impinge on his/her delivery, which should be engaged rather than robot-like, measured and clear.

6. That the newscaster will tend to look us apparently in the eye for at least most of the time. He/she will sit still and will delegate stories to special correspondents, when appropriate, who will take precedence over roving, junior reporters. While the latter may, just, have a regional accent, particularly if they are representing a regional television company, the newcaster will use received pronunciation and standard English.

These are just a start; pupils are usually only too willing to reveal their own opinions, that they trust a male newscaster more than a female one, that all news is boring, 'It's all about politics, nothing to do with us'. Many of these issues can be aired through simple exercises which even first year pupils can attempt:

Pupils might begin by trying to pin down 'news' by dividing into groups of four or five. Each group becomes the editorial panel for the BBC or ITV five forty five news; they will gather their news from the news agencies represented by the rest of the class. One member from each group visits each of the other groups in the classroom and collects three pieces of news from each. The news is real in the sense that it reflects things which have actually happened to the pupils in the course of the previous week, though some of it will be more newsworthy, less trivial than the rest. Once the editorial panel has gathered the news items, it is informed that it will only have the time to broadcast ten short items or eight longer ones, or an appropriate combination of the two types. The group must decide which stories it will discard immediately, and why, and which it will retain. It will also decide the order in which the news items will appear and will be required to justify the selection and order in

the plenary session in which each of the groups will
reveal the results of its deliberations. Alternatively, the news can be fed to the groups by the
teacher, who has noted the content of the previous
night's news broadcasts; the pupils' selections can
be compared with those actually televised. This
introductory exercise does not, of course, attempt
to reproduce the real pressures of working in such a
situation; it inevitably lacks context since pupils
are not aware of the content of accompanying and
preceding press, radio and television reports, nor
can it reproduce the implicit but nevertheless
powerful editorial and censorship pressures from
within the organisation. It does at least, though,
encourage pupils to articulate their own ideas of
what constitutes the news and goes some way towards
revealing the problematical nature of news gathering
and news reporting and paves the way for slightly
more ambitious exercises:

Here, individual pupils, working in different
areas, feed in items of news to Reuter's news-
gathering agency. Groups of pupils, representing
the news editorial team for ITN or BBC, collect the
news from the agency and sift through the contents
to locate and order the most significant items. The
teacher acts as a maverick, breaking news stories
sporadically in order to challenge pupils' decision
making abilities. The editorial groups have the
option of directing foreign and domestic reporters
back to the original sources to uncover and check
the details. This simulation is simple enough for
pupils to prepare the materials for themselves,
producing a quite detailed report of the original
news story, which is then summarised for distribution to the news agency. Analysis of real news
programmes will help pupils to devise their own
planning schedules for the editorial team, who will
be responsible for producing the finished news
script to be read by the newscaster. This sort of
exercise has important spin-offs for writing since
here summary has a purpose and context and is not
the disembodied assignment which is all too familiar
in classrooms. The summary is balanced by practice
in expansion, as correspondents, sent to the scene
of the news, return with more details. The finished
broadcast version can then, interestingly, be compared with the original detailed story which was
summarised for the news agency, constituting a form
of rather sophisticated Chinese Whispers and making
the point that much can happen to 'news' over the
passage of time and space, as it passes from one

mouth or pen to another.

As with the earlier exercise, attempting to crystallise the reasons why the editorial team have arrived at a certain order (or why they have disagreed) is an important part of the process. The exercise cannot realistically explore the impact of having film to accompany some stories and not others but, by assuming that they can get film for all but the stories which have just broken, pupils can begin to distinguish between stories which have an obvious pictorial appeal and those which can, acceptably, be described by the newscaster. They can explore the significance of vivid footage in boosting a news item to the top of the list. Pupils can gauge the effect on the perceived importance of a story by shifting its position in the schedule. They can explore their own assumptions about the way news should be read by trying some unorthodox studio approaches, beginning by listing the norms for reading the early evening or mid evening news in terms of dress, positioning, studio design and decor, body posture, pacing, tone, volume and thence explore what happens when one or more of these unwritten rules is flouted. For example, the newscaster might deliver the news in an open-necked shirt, sitting at an angle with his legs crossed, with no desk in sight and showing, however subtly, through tone and facial expression, his reaction to what he is reading. Pupils may care to contrast this with the well known comedy sketch in which the usually impassive and uninvolved sports reporter reads out the pools results, gradually becoming more euphoric as it appears that he stands to win the jackpot himself. His joy turns to desperation and grief as it gradually becomes clear that he has just missed out on a great win. Pupils may build up the level of divergent behaviour gradually, experimenting with different tones and volumes for different stories or key words, and altering a few carefully chosen words in the content to transform an apparently objective report into an altogether more biassed one. Groups may be given set briefs: 'Present the news in such a way that you indicate that the editorial team's sympathies lie with the "establishment", but not so obviously that you will be accused of bias'; 'Present the news in such a way that you make it clear that your sympathies lie with the man in the street'. Pupils may be challenged to achieve the apparently impossible, to take a very controversial and suspect speech given by a member of the royal family or senior member of parliament and present it

in a sympathetic light, or to take an unexceptional
speech delivered by a celebrity and to present it in
an outrageous or inflammatory light. These exercises lead naturally into the television interview,
a device often used to explore the news in an apparently open-ended way, but where the same processes
of selection and manipulation are involved in making, rather than simply delivering the message.

The Television Interview

It is sensible to begin by identifying what pupils
already know about the conventions associated with
the television interview, including the following
norms:

1. The interviewer is not expected to obtrude
   his or her own opinions but is there to encourage the interviewee to disclose as much
   as possible.
2. The interviewer represents another point of
   view to that of the person interviewed.
   This view will almost always be a personally uninvolved one, either:
   a. A neutral one, particularly where the
      interview deals with an uncontroversial
      subject, such as the return from a
      successful expedition.
   b. Devil's advocate, particularly where the
      point of view of the interviewee is the
      sensible consensus one, for example
      promoting the desirability of conserving
      woodlands.
   c. An establishment or consensus view where
      the interviewee's arguments are contro-
      versial and aberrant, for example, prom-
      oting an organisation such as Exit.
3. Interviewer and interviewee are normally
   seated, or less often standing, at the same
   level. The latter is often made to appear
   more prominent since it is hoped that he or
   she will do more of the talking.
4. The direction of the interview will normally be controlled by the interviewer,
   whose choice of questions can probe deeper
   or take the interview on to a new topic.
   Only the most self-confident and assertive
   interviewee will engineer the chance to
   control the course of the interview, sometimes turning the tables and questioning
   the interviewer.
5. Interviewees are not expected to refuse to

answer or walk away. (There have been some famous exceptions, including politicians and criminals, who have flouted this 'rule'.) Where there is a risk of this, 'no go' areas are normally negotiated in advance. As an alternative, politicians, in particular, are adept at fielding questions, fudging answers and transforming questions into the ones they wished to hear.

6. The most aggressive and probing interviewers are almost always male; Robin Day is a good example. Gone are the days when interviewers were almost exclusively male but even today there is an assumption that the bullying female is an unacceptable aberration.

Pupils can attempt to understand the artificial, choreographed nature of the apparently informal and unmanipulated interview, by exploring the processes involved for themselves. These are:

Research
Knowing what you want to know
Exploring the constraints
Framing the questions
Managing the interview

'Research' includes delving into the background and opinions of the interviewee and discovering more about the topics at issue. Pupils do not have access to tailor made archives and libraries in the same way that media journalists and researchers do, but they can exploit this as an exercise in developing library skills, particularly where they imagine they are interviewing a famous character from history or literature. It helps if pupils are given a key moment to focus upon, perhaps a blunder; the interviewee is then alerted to the fact that the interview will tend to concentrate upon this and warned that he will need to prepare his defence, aided by his researches. Historical blunders might include: Philip II of Spain being questioned upon the reasons for the Armada débâcle of 1588; Richard II interviewed about the sequence of events leading to his imprisonment; Napoleon questioned on St. Helena. These can be approached as two-pronged affairs, involving the English and history departments. The 'literary' interview can be used as a form of revision, inquiring into Hal's rejection of

Falstaff, Antonio's pledge to Shylock, Malvolio's
trust in the fabricated letter, and George's reasons for killing Lennie in 'Of Mice and Men'.
    While the research is in progress the inter-
viewer will already be narrowing down what he wants
to know; this can result in perhaps four or five
sub-areas, for example:

    Why did you not heed the warnings?
    Why did you trust someone who was unproven and
    likely to be hostile to your cause?
    Why did you delegate so much to inferiors?
    Why did you not accept an escape route when it
    was offered to you?

Few interviewers will feel able to ask such crudely
aggressive questions with impunity, even though they
might like to, and they will need to find more
subtle approaches to these 'pressure points'. The
interviewee, meanwhile, should be anticipating
these questions and preparing possible defence
strategies. Both participants will be anticipating
the constraints: obvious factors such as time, the
acceptability of certain questions and answers and
kinds of language, the prospective audience, and the
time of broadcast. Only then can the questions be
framed, perhaps distinguishing between the high
priority and low priority ones, and trying to anticipate possible answers and the direction in which
these may take the interview. The self-assured
interviewer may feel that areas for questioning are
sufficient support to see him through, but most will
appreciate the safety net of specific questions to
fall back on. All of these processes will have a
hand in deciding the overall tone of the interview
but much will also depend on the 'chemistry' of the
participants, since each will inevitably respond to
the stance and tone of the other, ensuring that any
interview is always an unpredictable entity.
    The interviewer's introductory remarks will be
very influential in suggesting his attitude to the
interviewee: 'Sir John (Falstaff), how pleasant to
see you looking so well...' (Informal, condescen-
ding, the inference being that he often looks
unwell); 'Sir John Falstaff - may I call you that? -
I'm sure our viewers would dearly love to know why
you should find yourself in the dire situation you
do...' (Deferential to the point of impertinent over
obsequiousness, trying to put a vain man off guard
and alerting the audience to the fact that Sir
John's behaviour is at odds with his title and

status and friendship with the future king. The interviewer is assuming that a 'dire situation' exists and hoping that this will inexorably lead Sir John and the audience to this assumption too. He is asking Falstaff to define the situation, thus pushing him further into the trap.)

It will inevitably help if pupils are able to watch and identify the techniques employed by skilled political interviewers, such as Brian Walden in ITV's 'Weekend World' and Robin Day in Radio 4's 'The World at One' and compare these with those used by late night chat show hosts and breakfast television interviewers. By recording their own interviews, pupils can identify the more successful and least successful moments, from the interviewer's and interviewee's standpoints, since, what makes for edifying or entertaining viewing may be disastrous as far as one of the participants is concerned. Just as pastiche and parody can help to locate characteristics of literary style, so exaggeration or concentration on certain elements can expose interview techniques. Pupils may work in threes, where one is the director, one interviewee and one interviewer. The director feeds the interviewer a specific brief, such as one of the following:

'Hold him up for public scorn.'
'Help her unwind sufficiently to tell as much as possible of her story.'
'Encourage him to criticise his colleagues.'
'Trap her into contradiction.'
'Approach the interview as though you are the man in the street seeking information from the expert.'
'Conduct the interview as a representative of a major American television channel, presenting a report on quaint British customs.'

Few pupils will be able to explore the decisive influence of editing in reinforcing and transforming the messages that emerge from a television interview, but they can come closer to such an understanding by producing a radio 'vox pop' programme based on a local and preferably contentious issue, in which pupils take to the street to gather the views of as representative a sample as possible of local people. A dramatised rehearsal, in the classroom or hall, will help to demonstrate some of the problems latent in such an exercise. Pupils can identify these for themselves and document them on separate cards:

The person who - disdains all knowledge of the
subject and rushes off.
exploits the opportunity to show
off, acting the expert.
goes off at a tangent.
exploits the opportunity to publicise another issue.
is genuinely well-informed and
interested.
is shy and self-conscious.
insists on asking the interviewer
questions.
insists, 'You're joking mate,
aren't you? This is "Going for a
Laugh."'

The High Street is simulated and the interviewer
stops the pupils who are playing the passers by, in
turn, unaware of which types they represent. He
tries his hardest to encourage each speaker to
express their views succinctly, without wasting the
time allotted to the assignment. Afterwards, the
interviewer, passers by and audience discuss the
successes and failures and try to assess the extent
to which this is a realistic anticipation of the
problems they may meet in their homes, village or
town. The class may try out its interviewing techniques in the school, during the dinner hour, or may
go out into the community during lesson time or may
conduct the interviews at home, using their own
equipment. They may be told in advance that, as far
as possible, the interviewer's questions will be
deleted from the final version and transcript, to
produce a collage of juxtaposed views, representing
as many sides as possible of the arguments. The
editing and compilation, crude though this will be
without professional equipment, should make clear
the scope the editor has for rearrangement and for
the suppression of some views and the reinforcement
of others. Some pupils, working in pairs or groups,
may choose to demonstrate this by working from the
transcript and judiciously slicing and rearranging
the content to produce a picture biassed for the
proposition, or against it. The exercise should
demonstrate why there are not more vox pop programmes on television and it should also encourage
pupils to look more closely at those sections of
'That's Life' and regional magazine programmes which
allow ordinary people to speak out, too often about
trivial subjects. Much of what the pupils record
will be inconsequential and unusable and, given the

importance of entertaining the audience, the more
profound but duller comments may have to be omitted
in favour of the more controversial or ridiculous
parts.

The Television Documentary Play

The television documentary play is becoming increasingly influential in conveying powerful messages
about the 'state of society'. The impact of 'Cathy
Come Home' or, more recently, 'The Boys from the
Black Stuff' and 'Walter', demonstrate why this
should be so; facts that never make the news ironic-
ally just because they affect large numbers of so-
called ordinary people, can be presented in a suitably condensed and shaped form so that they educate
as they entertain, and in such a way that the events
engage the audience's emotions. While statistics
can be disregarded since they are disembodied, a
suffering individual, with whom we identify, can
move us to protest.

Pupils need to understand the extent to which
documentary plays are artefacts, as much well made
plays as their fellows that do not take on current
social issues. What all documentary plays have in
common, of course, is some basis in fact, either
through their concentration on real people, as in
Elaine Morgan's 'The Life and Times of Lloyd George'
or in focussing on current phenomena, as in David
Leland's 'Rhino' which vividly portrayed society's
irrational victimisation of a school truant. Devising a documentary play is rather like starting a
PhD; both require that the writer is really interested in what he is investigating. Pupils, ideally
working in groups, must come to the project enthusiastically, whether they pick up another's suggestion or initiate one themselves. Historical topics
are in some ways easier to develop since there is
usually ample source material, and biographical
series such as Hamlyn's 'The Life and Times of...'
make the task much simpler. More topical issues
such as the social dilemmas faced by some second
generation Asian girls, or one eighteen year old's
fight to look after his orphaned brothers and sisters single-handed, are more difficult to sustain
unless they come close to the writer's experiences.

As with interviews, the extent to which documentary plays can be shaped to produce quite different views of issues or personalities (since neutral-
ity is impossible) can be demonstrated with the aid
of historical characters whose lives are already
well documented. Pupils can select and research a

personality with a view in mind, perhaps intending
to show the private side to the public face or demonstrating how he or she owed fame less to genius
and more to the irresistible tide of accident and
history (as in Brecht's 'The Resistible Rise of
Arturo Ui'). Monologues may be delivered by carefully chosen characters from the subject's life and
times, to reinforce the chosen view, or views, and
as a way into a more fully developed dramatisation.
Groups of pupils can select those events, characters, comments and scenes which will bolster their
thesis; these can be shaped to form a simple scenario. Where the whole class, in groups, has been
working on the same character or issue, this is the
moment to compare some of these scenarii, to see the
extent to which a different overall view has decided
the selection of scenes and characters and the
course of the play. A sample of scenes can be
improvised and, or scripted; pupils should not be
too inhibited by anxieties over strict historical
accuracy since this is intended as an exploration of
a particular genre rather than a history test.
Given sufficient commitment, one or more scenarii
may form the basis for a class, even a school play.
Once pupils have tried their hands at shaping their
own documentary plays they can relate their efforts
to similar television offerings, comparing them with
documentaries and 'Plays for Today', and watching a
documentary together in order to identify the ways
in which the materials have been arranged in ways
which mediate 'the truth', bringing it closer to the
documentary play than to true fly on the wall reporting.

The Local Radio Station
This aspect of the mass media deserves particular
attention, since, in an era of poor facilities for
broadcasting pupils' own work within schools, it
offers real opportunities for pupils to see their
own work reach a wider audience and to be taken
seriously by discriminating professionals. While it
is not, of course, unknown for pupils' work to find
its way into educational television, it is far more
likely that any direct relationship between broadcasting and the classroom will develop via local
radio stations, just because of their accessibility.
Many local radio stations are happy, given sufficient warning and suitably restricted numbers, to
allow pupils to see them at work. This may be
enough to suggest some of the general characteristics that television, radio, and the press share:

the stranglehold imposed by constricted schedules, the lack of time to meditate and reconsider at length, the importance of trying to determine priorities, and what will entertain, and the need for flexibility, often a euphemism for working long hours when circumstances demand.

Local radio, more so than any other of the media, sees the public as both consumers and providers, contributors to phone-ins, vox pop programmes, and contributors of ideas and the content for programmes. Those local radio stations lucky enough to have an educational producer, make educational programmes which rival in quality the networked productions of BBC Radio 4. Local programmes span an audience which includes the interested layman and parents, teachers and pupils from the playgroup and nursery school through to the technical college and university. One station's 'English' output suggests the diversity of this offering to listeners:

Speaking Up: A continuing series in which small groups of speakers from local schools accept the challenge of ten minutes of airtime to present topics of their choice reflecting some of their school and community-based interests.

Tales out of School: A continuing series in which young writers in local secondary schools read from their original narrative work. Each of the ten minute programmes has a selection of readings from an individual school and illustrates a range of themes and approaches which have prompted lively written work.

Listening to the Words: In which a local teacher exercises his ear on the words from popular songs that are often taken for granted. The programmes raise many points suitable for further discussion by students and older pupils.

You Write to Say: A series featuring writing received from local listeners and designed to share this with a wider readership than that of the school or college magazine.

This BBC local radio station, like many more, is always prepared to consider pupils' work for broadcast, if it is of a suitably high standard, whether it fits a predesigned slot or not. Local radio can

be a significant agent in the cycle of creativity,
where the station's output both stimulates, and is
stimulated by, pupils' own work. One example may
help to demonstrate how pupils, their teachers, the
station and its listeners can gain through this
cycle:

'Gawain and the Green Knight'. As part of their
English work, the whole of the first year in a local
comprehensive school has been studying the theme
'Journeys'. The final focus for this theme is to be
the Middle English narrative poem, 'Gawain and the
Green Knight'. This has been chosen, not simply
because of its literary interest, but because of the
opportunities it offers for associated drama work.
By the time the idea of a dramatisation of this is
first introduced to the pupils, they have already
read a prose paraphrase, have compared this with
some of the original and have an inkling of the
course of the narrative. The pupils are invited to
audition for the major roles: Sir Gawain, Sir
Bertilak or the Green Knight, King Arthur, Queen
Guinevere and Sir Bertilak's lady. One of the
advantages of the poem is that the cast list can be
stretched to fit those interested in taking part;
many will be involved as knights, ladies, jesters,
porters and servants at King Arthur's and Sir
Bertilak's courts and minor characters can justifiably be written in, if required. At least six
pupils will act as narrators, reading from a modifi-
cation of the Penguin paraphrase[16], the product of a
collaboration between a teacher and a small group of
pupils. Suitable early English music will be played
as an overlay for some of the movement sequences and
to accompany Sir Gawain's journeys. None of the
characters will need to learn a script since, once
the class is clear of what happens and why, the
emphasis will be on improvisation, on trying to feel
as the character must have felt and anticipating
what he or she would have said and done in the
situation. Informal 'rehearsals' take place at
weekly intervals in the lunch hour during the summer
term. Only the hunting and the fight sequences are
tightly choreographed, in order to avoid confusion,
given the large cast involved.
        A performance given to the local primary school
comes closest to a formal 'dress rehearsal'. The
pupils are aware that the final performance will be
the excuse for a summer term day out, since the
entire first year and their English teachers will
travel to the Roaches area of the Peak District,

thought by some scholars to be the Gawain poet's
site for the final meeting with the Green Knight.
Here the performance will take the better part of a
day, with the cast and audience progressing from one
acting place to another amid the magnificent scen-
ary, and recreating Gawain's journey from Camelot to
the Green Knight's lair, high in the mossy darkness
of Lud's Chapel. A local radio producer will be
present to record the proceedings, with an explanatory running commentary which describes the scene as
the players, in full Medieval costume, move through
the trees to take up their positions. The scenes
are photographed by staff and pupils to make a pictorial collage which will be displayed in the school.
    The recording of the finished product is both a
goal and an ending, and a beginning. It will be a
stimulus within the school for associated work and
future English and drama projects; it is proof
positive of a creatively satisfying and successful
undertaking and, when broadcast, it will reinforce
both staff's and pupils' confidence in their own
organisational and dramatic capabilities. The
broadcast will also suggest dramatic possibilities
to other teachers, other pupils. This is reinforced
by placing the recording of the final performance in
perspective. It is introduced by excerpts from some
of the rehearsals, demonstrating how the improvisation was built up in stages, relying as much as
possible on pupils' own ideas; it ends with a post
mortem delivered by participating pupils and staff
which underlines the kinds of learning that have
taken place, learning which concerns not just a
single poem but which is related to the techniques
of broadcasting, group co-operation, voice projec-
tion, the pacing of words, movement in full costume,
and much more besides.

COMMUNICATIONS COURSES AND 'BASIC SKILLS' COURSES

Communications and Basic Skills courses are normally
associated with colleges of further education,
since, despite the suggestions made in the 'N' and
'F' proposals[17] and the existence of 'O' and 'A'
Level courses in Communication Studies[18], schools
have tended to talk in terms of English as literature, for the most part. The Schools Council 16-19
Project[19] was not alone in calling for a recognition
of the need for a changing definition of English for
the 1980s. This would entail a broadening of English examination syllabi to suit all students, and
not simply the tiny minority preparing for single

honours courses at university. It would demand a
recognition of the importance of drama and media
studies as integral components of 'English', rather
than as arbitrary appendages. Examination boards
are already having to redefine their aims in a
decade in which the school leaving age is rising
inexorably in response to unemployment, to seven-
teen, and will continue to rise as pre-vocational
courses become the norm for the vast majority of
sixteen year olds. The Youth Training Scheme,
introduced officially in September 1983, for sixteen
year old school leavers, acknowledges the importance
of communication skills, in addition to work experience and off the job training. Teachers of English
are responding to these initiatives; most can claim,
with a clear conscience, that by advancing on a
broad curricular front which acknowledges the importance of pupils' own communication skills and which
helps them to interpret the products of others, they
are currently fitting students for the complex
demands of life beyond school.

Any definition of English must be broad enough
to encompass the two poles of communication and
interpretation, from 'basic skills' at one end to
literature at the other:

> There are two poles, as it were, in communica-
> tion and thinking. Towards the one end stud-
> ents are thinking of "functional success" in
> coping with specific, everyday experiences of
> getting things done...But there is the other
> pole, concerned...with appreciation and under-
> standing of other people and oneself, and with
> notions of how society around one actually
> works. Language towards this pole is a medium
> for developing awareness, interpreting the life
> we encounter and reflecting on it.[20]

Any broadening of the definition of English must
reflect the importance of communication and thus the
mass media, and any interpretation of communication
must take account of drama. Drama has a particular
role to play in developing the 'functional' communication skills, a fact which certificated communications courses have recognised for some time. The
general objectives for the popular City and Guilds
Certificate in Communication Skills (Level One)
suggest the contribution that drama, and particularly role play and simulation, can make. For
example:

Receive and Interpret Information in Oral Form

1. Listen to and understand information in
   oral form
   a. Identify the relevant points from oral
      messages
2. Listen to and understand questions and
   requests
3. Identify statements which are/are not
   supported by evidence within a given situation
   a. Distinguish fact from opinion
   b. Identify emotive words and phrases
   c. Identify ambiguous or confusing state-
      ments...

Communicate Effectively in Oral Form

1. Organise content and communicate effectively
   a. Speak audibly
   b. Explain and describe objects/processes/
      events/opinions in a logical sequence
      or, where there is no strict logical
      requirement, sensibly and clearly.
2. Formulate questions and requests for a
   specific purpose.

The links between these objectives and Joan Tough's
classification of language uses[21] are obvious, and
the coursework assignments which require students
to put themselves into the position of another and
use language in a clear, constructive and imaginative manner, further reinforce the relationship
between drama, communication skills and English:

> The Students' Union Committee is offering to
> provide the initial deposit you need to get the
> disco organised. You must therefore provide
> them with enough information for them to choose
> one of the programmes as worthy of their sup-
> port. Task Two is to speak to the Students'
> Union Committee outlining both the programmes
> you have drawn up in Task One and giving rea-
> sons for their selection. Record what you say
> on the tape recorder.

How we label this sort of work is irrelevant,
whether as Communications, Basic Skills, Survival
Skills or Drama, so long as we recognise that it
falls within the sphere of English teaching at its

best, for,

> Good drama teaching and good English teaching
> share the same essential purposes, aiming to
> cultivate children's powers of responsive
> imagination, in order that they may grasp "the
> reality of human speech, behaviour and emo-
> tions" with growing sense and sensitivity; and
> aiming to develop powers of communication. In
> the best work these purposes are rarely separ-
> able.[22]

It may well be that the best way to reinforce the
importance of drama in the curriculum, in the
future, will be to publicise the opportunities it
provides for enabling pupils to 'practise' - using
James Britton's definition[23] - those communication
skills they will need beyond school, thus creating a
pre-vocational course in its broadest and most
enlightened form.

NOTES

1. F.R. Leavis and Denys Thompson, Culture
and Environment: The Training of Critical Awareness
(Chatto and Windus, 1942).
2. Richard Hoggart, 'Culture: Dead and Alive'
in Speaking to Each Other, Vol.1, About Society
(Chatto and Windus, 1970).
3. Michael Marland, 'Mainstream' in Denys
Thompson (ed.), Directions in the Teaching of English (Cambridge University Press, 1969).
4. H. Himmelweit et al, Television and the
Child (Oxford University Press, 1958).
5. Graham Murdock and Guy Phelps, Mass Media
and the Secondary School, a report from the Schools
Council Project on Mass Media and the Secondary
School (Macmillan, 1973).
6. John Dixon et al, Education 16-19: The Role
of English and Communication, Schools Council 16-19
Project (Macmillan, 1979).
7. The Newsom Report, Half Our Future, Ministry of Education (HMSO, 1963).
8. See 5.
9. Len Masterman, Teaching About Television
(Macmillan, 1980).
10. Sue Horner (ed.), Best Laid Plans: English
Teachers at Work, a report for the Secondary Committee of the National Association for the Teaching of
English (Longman, 1983).
11. See, for example, The Mass Media series,

R.B. Heath: Sounds and Images (Radio, Television, Cinema), The Popular Press (Newspapers, Magazines, Paperbacks), The Persuaders (Advertising), Nelson, 1975, regularly reprinted.

12. The Newbolt Report, The Teaching of English in England (HMSO, 1921).

13. See 6.

14. The Sunday Times, 10 July 1983.

15. See 9.

16. Sir Gawain and the Green Knight, translated by Brian Stone (Penguin, 1959).

17. The Schools Council N and F proposals for the reform of sixth form curricula and examinations (1977).

18. See The Oxford Examining Board's 'O' Level in Modern Communications (with special reference to television) and the Associated Examining Board's 'A' Level in Communication Studies.

19. See 6.

20. Ibid.

21. Joan Tough, Talk for Teaching and Learning, Schools Council Communications Skills Project, 7-13 (Ward Lock Educational, 1979).

22. Christopher Parry, 'Drama', in Directions in the Teaching of English, see 3.

23. James Britton, Language and Learning (Penguin, 1970).

DRAMA AND THE ENGLISH THEME

'NOAH'

Cast
Noah
God
Noah's Wife
Noah's Eldest Son   (married to)   First Wife
Noah's Second Son   (married to)   Second Wife
Noah's Third Son   (married to)   Third Wife

(Noah, alone, prays to God)
NOAH: Might God, creator of everything that exists,
listen to me, please. I'm very worried because
everywhere I turn I see nothing but sin and wickedness. Some people are proud, some quick to anger
and some are greedy and lazy. I don't claim to be a
goody-goody but I have tried to keep your command-
ments and now I'm scared you'll take it out on the
lot of us, me included. I ask you - is that fair?
(God speaks from above)
GOD: Since I have made everything on earth, from the
greatest emperor to the smallest wriggly worm, I
have always asked man to live according to my laws
and worship me alone. Instead he's gone round
sinning, left, right and centre. I wish to goodness
I'd never made you all in the first place, but
what's done is done and now you must suffer. I
shall flood the earth and kill every living creature
...
NOAH: But you can't...
GOD: Don't interrupt. Anyhow how would you know
what I can and can't do? Where was I? Oh yes, I
was just about to say that you and all your family -
that's if you can keep them quiet for long enough -
will build a great ship, three hundred cubits long
and fifty cubits wide and you will sail on the flood

waters to safety. Make sure you have plenty of room
ℛ in the hold because you must squeeze in two of every
kind of living creature as well as all the stores
and groceries you'll need for such a long journey.
You must start this straight away, there's not a
moment to lose!
NOAH: Would you believe it? To think he noticed and
now he's going to save us. But perhaps I'm just
hearing voices (he bangs the sides of his head) and
it's not God at all...
GOD (losing patience): Well I haven't got time to
prove it to you now, just take my holy word for it -
and get on with that ship! (Exit God)
(Noah approaches his wife)
WIFE: Where on earth have you been? We women might
as well be dead as far as you men are concerned.
You're always ignoring me.
NOAH: I've got a lot of things on my mind.
WIFE: Oh don't try that one, you've got nothing up
top to worry with...I often wonder what I ever saw
in you, you're always whining about something.
(She turns to the women in the audience)
Take my word for it women, if you want a quiet life,
don't get married. Men are more trouble than
they're worth.
NOAH: Shut your mouth Wife, or I'll shut it for you.
WIFE: Don't try to threaten me or you'll get what's
coming to you...
(Noah tries to grab her but she dodges him and gets
him in an arm lock)
NOAH (desperate, breathless): OK, OK, you win...this
time. God must of had an off day when he made you
...thank God I don't have to take two of you into
the ark.
WIFE (suspicious): What was that about an ark?
NOAH: Call in the rest of them and I'll tell you all
at once...
WIFE (bellows): Children!...Michael...Alan...Tracey
...Sandy...Erroll...Bren...Where have they got to?
Skiving off again I expect...(they slowly arrive)
NOAH (in one breath): Wife and children listen carefully to me I've got something important to say we
must all escape from this place before the rains
come in the ark with two of everything on earth and
it's got to be three hundred cubits wide and fifty
cubits long...or is it the other way round?
WIFE: What ark? What rains?...What rubbish. Didn't
I tell you all he had a screw loose? Here he goes
with another crazy plan...
ELDEST SON: It didn't say anything on the weather
forecast about rain...just sunny periods and...

NOAH: I am speaking the truth. God told me. He's
going to flood the earth and drown everything
except you and me and the creatures we're taking
with us. It's a punishment because everyone's been
up to no good.
WIFE (quite impressed): So you weren't grovelling in
the dirt, planting greens, you must have been lis-
tening to God.
NOAH: He told us to hurry up...
SECOND SON: Look a flash of lightning...
NOAH: Follow me, we must find wood...and all those
animals!
(The family build the ark and collect pairs of crea-
tures)
(Noah comes to the front to talk to his wife who is
sulking and refuses to do any work at all)
NOAH: The animals are all aboard, don't you keep us
waiting, wife.
WIFE: That's the funniest ark I've ever seen, and
I'm not going in with any smelly animals.
(She starts knitting)
NOAH: Look at the skies! Feel the rain!
FIRST WIFE: Please Mother, come in quickly. We may
never see the sun again.
SECOND WIFE: Just hear the wind howling...
WIFE: That's just your father's stomach rumbling...
THIRD WIFE: We've got just the place for you to knit
on board, Mum.
WIFE: Ugh! Just look at this water.
NOAH: Yes it'll be up to your knees if you don't
come now...and anyway who's going to cook, look
after us...there's no one who can cook chips like
you...
WIFE: Alright, alright, don't go on...but don't ask
me to clean out those animals.
(She climbs into the ark and the gang-plank is
pulled up)
NOAH: Thank God you're in. Now you're here you'll
take orders from me, I'm Captain and if you don't
watch your lip we'll shove you out on a raft.
(Wife creeps up behind him and tries to throttle
him. He escapes and chases her inside the ark.
Sounds of fighting. He comes out, rubbing his
bruises)
NOAH (he holds a line over the side of the ark): Now
I'll test the water. See, it's a long way to the
bottom. Not surprising when you think it's been
raining for forty days.
WIFE: Give me a go. I've run out of knitting wool.
Thought you said it was a long way - look...
NOAH: Cor, the water's going down.

182

WIFE: Any fool could tell you that...look isn't that the top of the Post Office Tower?

THIRD SON: We must be sailing over Buckingham Palace ...

WIFE: Let's hope the weather hasn't spoilt all those nice rooms.

(The family race round the ark noticing all sorts of sights as the water goes down)

NOAH: (he falls to his knees, tired out) Well God you kept your word, we're all safe and the creatures have come through...

WIFE: I bet he didn't say anything about them all breeding like rabbits did he?

NOAH: I might of known you'd spoil it with your crude comments. Don't you see this is a very special moment, like you see in films.

WIFE (impressed): Perhaps they'll write about us, make a film about us...

NOAH: They? Our kids'll have to do it if anyone - we're the only ones left.

WIFE: I hadn't thought about that. It makes us even more special doesn't it?

ELDEST SON: Yes, and lucky, that God saved us.

(They are nearly knocked over as the ark hits dry land)

FIRST WIFE: We've landed!

NOAH: Now the real work is starting.

WIFE: Hey, if there aren't any more shops where am I going to get some more wool?

NOAH: Better go and make friends with those sheep.

(The Wife starts to make a run at him but is caught in the act and turns it into a hug)

WIFE: Just for once I think you're right.

INDEX